Titles in the series:

Company Law

Constitutional Law

Contract Law

Criminal Law

Employment Law

English Legal System

European Community Law

Evidence

Family Law

GCSE Law

Jurisprudence

Land Law

Medical Law

Succession

Tort

Trusts

ESSENTIAL GCSE LAW

Kenny Chin
Solicitor

Routledge
Taylor & Francis Group

LONDON AND NEW YORK

Foreword

This book is part of the Cavendish Essential series. The books in the series are designed to provide useful revision aids for the hard-pressed student. They are not, of course, intended to be substitutes for more detailed treatises. Other textbooks in the Cavendish portfolio must supply these gaps.

Each book in the series follows a uniform format of a checklist of the areas covered in each chapter, followed by expanded treatment of 'Essential' issues looking at examination topics in depth.

The team of authors bring a wealth of lecturing and examining experience to the task in hand. Many of us can even recall what it was like to face law examinations!

Professor Nicholas Bourne AM
General Editor, Essential Series
Conservative Member for Mid and West Wales

Preface

The purpose of this book is to provide a revision aid for students who study GCSE law. It can also be used as an introductory text at the start of the course, from which students can expand their understanding of various topics by referring to materials provided by their teachers or in more detailed textbooks.

The book is divided into three main parts. The first part covers the nature of law and modern sources of English law. The second part describes various laws in practice, including criminal law, contract, tort, family law, law of succession and freedom under the law. After students have studied what law is, where our law comes from and various specific areas of the law, part three explains criminal and civil procedures and by whom the laws are administered. All three parts combine to cover most GCSE Law syllabuses which, in my opinion, give good coverage of various aspects of law and provide an excellent first step for students who are thinking of building their career, or are simply interested, in law. Attempts are made in this book to present the material in plain English and to explain some complicated legal issues in easy to understand language. It is hoped that this book can help students find more enjoyment in studying the course and to be successful in examinations.

My thanks are due to my father-in-law, Cliff Parkin, and my wife, Carol, for their support and advice.

I have endeavoured to state the law as at July 2000.

Kenny Chin
July 2000

Table of Contents

1 Nature of Law

You should be familiar with the following areas:

- what is law and how it is distinguished from moral rules?
- why does society need law?
- why does the law need changing?
- what is the classification of law?
- what is the difference between civil and criminal cases?

What is law?

Law is:

(a)   rules of conduct;

(b)   which the State treats as binding;

(c)   backed by sanctions;

(d)   obligatory within the community;

(e)   controlling the activities of the people towards each other and their relationship with the State.

Moral rules are also rules of conduct guiding the behaviour of people. The main difference between legal and moral rules is that legal rules are enforceable by the State, but moral rules are not. If a person has committed a criminal offence, he can be put into prison or ordered to pay a fine. If he is found liable under a civil law suit, he may be ordered by the court to pay compensation or to stop doing something which he should not do (that is, an injunction order). But if the person has been selfish and inconsiderate without breaking any law, he may be disliked by others, but the State will not place any sanction against him.

Some examples of moral and legal rules

Moral rules	Where moral and legal rules meet	Pure legal rules
– Be honest	– Stealing	– Some traffic regulations
– Do not be selfish	– Assault and battery	– Many company laws
– Act on one's promise	– Breach of contract	– Rules regarding the validity of
	– Murder	a will

In many cases, moral and legal rules overlap. Murder and stealing are not only morally wrong, but are also criminal offences. When a person has entered into a contract with another, he is morally as well as legally obliged to fulfil the agreement.

Why society needs law and why law needs changing

Human beings are social animals and we live in communities. No person is perfect and we can do wrong. Some wrong doings are so serious that laws are introduced to prevent them. Law also combats problems and cures injustice. Some laws are pure legal rules which provide a system or code of practice for the members of society. The law requires motorists in the UK to drive on the left side of the road while other countries may do otherwise. Law directly, or indirectly, should also help to improve the quality of life of the people. As a result, people live and work together in an orderly and peaceful manner and individual rights and freedoms are protected.

Law needs changing all the time:

- *To reflect the values and public opinion of the people in the society*

  Public attitude can change, brought about by education, material prosperity, new ideas, experience of problems and contact with foreign countries. In a democratic society, law is constantly changing to reflect the changes in values and opinions of the majority and, sometimes, to protect the rightful interests of the minority.

- *To overcome problems*

  When a problem occurs which harms innocent people frequently and becomes serious, new law has to be introduced to prevent it from happening again. For an example, when stalking became more widespread in the mid-1990s, many victims (including the late Princess Diana, amongst many high profile celebrities and ordinary people) suffered disappointment because the courts found it difficult to convict stalkers under the law at that time. There was an outcry against such anti-social behaviour and public opinion demanded that new law be introduced to stop stalking at early stages. The government picked up this public view and brought about the Protection From Harassment Act 1997, which provides opportunities to convict a stalker long before serious harm is done. Because late payments caused detrimental effects on many small businesses, the Late Payment of Commercial Debts (Interest) Act 1998 was enacted to confer statutory entitlement to businesses to charge interest of 8% above base rate against late payments. The first phase was introduced in November 1998, enabling small businesses to charge interest against big companies. At a later stage, the law will ultimately be applicable to all businesses.

- *To cure 'injustice'*

  The courts are bound to follow established legal principles, but, sometimes, they experience situations when they have to decide matters which may be legally correct, but surely unjust. Such a problem can arise from obsolete previous judgments or from badly drafted legislation. In the circumstances, new law or regulations are required to overrule them. For instance, the Wills Act 1837 provided that there should be at least two witnesses to a will and a gift contained in the will to a witness would fail. The purpose was to have at least two witnesses who could testify as to the authenticity of the testator's signature and, if a witness was a beneficiary, there might be a conflict of interest and the witness may not acquire any benefit under the will. However, in *Re Bravda's Estate* (1968), there were three witnesses and the third witness was also a beneficiary. Although the purpose of the 1837 Act was fulfilled, the court was bound to follow the rule to decide that the third witness could not benefit from the gift. The Act which gave rise to this unjust situation was quickly amended by the Wills Act 1968, which provides that, as long as there are two witnesses who are not beneficiaries, it is sufficient. Any further witnesses who are beneficiaries can keep their gifts.

• *To improve social systems and to meet current needs*

Much business law, welfare law, criminal justice law and financial legislation (for example, the Chancellor of the Exchequer's budgets) provide social systems for the society. They keep changing for the purpose of improving the systems and of providing for current and on going revenue needs. There is now much legislation which is made to harmonise various systems with the rest of Europe. For example, the Trade Marks Act 1993 and the Commercial Agents (Council Directive) Regulations 1993, which unify trade marks and commercial agency laws throughout the Member States in the European Union.

Classification of law

There are many ways to classify law. The following chart shows one of the ways:

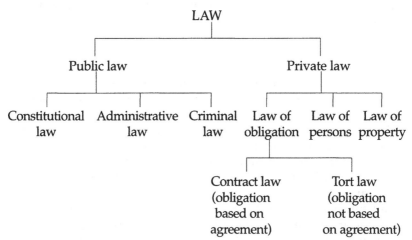

Constitutional law

Determines the functions of the principal organs of government and regulates their structures and their relationship with each other and with the citizens.

Administrative law

Relates to public administration. It is concerned with how powers are delegated to various organs of government, how administrative actions are controlled and checked and how public authorities may be liable to individuals.

Criminal law

Characterises certain unlawful acts and defaults as offences against the public and punishable by the State.

Private law

In a different context, private law is called civil law, which is concerned with the rights, duties and relationships of individuals or groups of individuals (for example, companies which are separate legal persons from their directors and shareholders, meaning that they can sue, be sued and own properties) towards each other.

Law of obligation

Includes contract law and tort. When there is a legal obligation, there is a duty and vice versa. A person will incur civil liability if he is in breach of that duty. In contract, such obligation is created by agreement reached between the parties. Tort is a French word, meaning civil wrong. In tort, the obligation is imposed by law. Members of a society living together have mutual duties to take care and not to harm each other. There is no need to have an agreement to set out those duties and, if a person's conduct falls below a reasonable standard of care and causes harm to others, then he is liable to civil remedies.

Law of persons

Includes law of succession and family law.

Law of property

Determines the nature and extent of the rights which individuals may enjoy over land and other properties.

Comparison between criminal and civil matters brought to the court

	Criminal	Civil
Parties to the action	R: Regina/Rex, Crown, the State; DPP: Director of Public Prosecutions; AG: Attorney General or other administrative authorities v Defendant (or accused)	Claimant (formerly, plaintiff); Applicant (eg, off/on licence applicant) or petitioner (eg, divorce petitioner) v Defendant (against a claimant) or respondent (against an applicant or petitioner)
Action	Prosecute	Sue, apply or petition
Purpose	Punish/reform offenders Protect society	Seek for remedies including damages, injunction, specific performance, etc
Courts of first instance	Magistrates' court then may transfer to Crown Court for trial by jury	County court or High Court
Burden of proof (we are discussing the proof of evidence and facts here, not the law)	Prosecution to prove beyond reasonable doubt. When there is reasonable doubt, then the jury must acquit	Claimant to prove on a balance of probabilities (that is, more than 50%). If a judge believes that a party has presented more proof than the other has, he will apply the law on the facts in which he believes and then make a decision

2 Modern Sources of English Law

You should be familiar with the following areas:

- **the process of how a Bill becomes a Statute**

- **supremacy of Parliament under the influence of European law**

- **various forms of delegated legislation, its criticism and justification**

- **the control of delegated legislation by Parliament and the courts**

- **various doctrine and rules of the common law system**

- **advantages and disadvantages of the common law system**

- **various forms of European law and their effect on English law**

Introduction

One special feature when studying law is that we not only need to know the law itself but where it comes from. When we answer a question in a law examination, we do not only set out the relevant law and apply it; we should also quote authorities to support our arguments, as lawyers would do when arguing their case in court. An authority may be a section in a statute, a legal regulation made by a government department, a case or a piece of European law. English law comes from four major sources:

(a) Acts of Parliament, that is, law made by enactment;

(b) delegated legislation;

(c) case law, that is, law made by judges;

(d) European Community law.

Acts of Parliament

This law making process is sometimes referred to as legislation or statutory law. Legislation is a body of rules which are formally enacted by the Houses of Parliament. Parliament is said to be omnipotent, it can overrule a law previously made by a judge and it can repeal its own previous statutes by passing a new Act. It is important in a democratic country that the citizens are governed by those whom we elect and the ultimate power and responsibility of legislation is placed on them. Until recently, there were approximately 1,200 members in the House of Lords, however, this number has been reduced due to reforms in the House. There are approximately 660 Members of Parliament (MPs) in the House of Commons. Members of Parliament are elected representatives from constituencies all over the UK and the main power of making and unmaking law falls on this House. Before an Act is passed by both Houses of Parliament and endorsed by the Monarch, the draft of law is called a Bill.

Types of Bill

There are three main types of Bill:
(a)   Public Bills;
(b)   Private Member's Bills;
(c)   Private Bills.

Public Bills

After a general election, the majority party in the House of Commons forms the government, which introduces Bills to be enacted to become law. These are Public Bills which are usually drafted by appropriate government departments. Since a statute is passed by a majority vote and the government introduces Public Bills, they are normally enacted without much difficulty, except for a few which meet strong opposition in the House of Lords.

Private Member's Bills

Each year, there is a ballot amongst the members of Parliament who wish to introduce legislation privately for certain issues of importance to them. However, time is limited in each session of Parliament and, normally, the responsibility of having the Bill drafted is placed on the proposer, therefore, unless a Bill is backed by the government, there is little chance of it becoming law. There are very few Bills which are enacted this way; however, one good exception is the Murder (Abolition of Death Penalty) Act 1965 introduced by Mr Sidney Silverman. Another type of Private Member's Bill (some authors may prefer to classify these as Private Bills) are those introduced by MPs under the so called 'ten minute' rule. With prior arrangement, an MP may speak in favour of the introduction of a Bill for ten minutes in the House. Very few of these speeches result in statutes, but they do serve the purpose of attracting attention from other legislators and the public to certain issues.

Private Bills (Local Bills)

These are Bills which are sponsored by local authorities or other public bodies such as public utility companies, banks and universities. They are designed to alter the legal position of the sponsor to enable them to provide a service to the public or to do so more efficiently. Some of them deal with matters such as building or alteration of roads, bridges, ports, waterworks, etc, while others aim to extend the powers of the sponsors which are concerned with the provision of public services such as gas, electricity, railways, etc.

Procedure

The table overleaf shows the most common procedure of how a Bill is enacted:

First Reading:	Formal introduction of a Bill to Parliament, usually by the minister concerned with the subject matter. The presentation is very brief. The Bill is then printed and published.
Second Reading:	The Bill is explained to the House when a general debate concerning it takes place, usually voting at the end.
Committee Stage:	This is when a clause by clause consideration of the Bill takes place. The committee can be a Select Committee specifically selected for the Bill, the Standing Committee which is appointed to examine Public Bills generally or the whole House. Amendments of the Bill are made at this stage.
Report Stage:	The Committee informs the House of the changes. Decisions take place and amendments may be added.
Third Reading:	The Bill is reviewed in its final form. There is normally a debate followed by formal voting. When passed, the Bill will be sent to the other House where a similar process from First Reading to Third Reading will take place.

Generally, Bills are passed in the Commons, first, then in the Lords. Sometimes, for the purpose of time saving or organisation of the legislation programme, less controversial Bills may pass through the House of Lords first. Presuming that a Bill has been passed in the Commons, there are alternative situations and one possible exceptional outcome after the Bill has been sent to the Lords:

(1) The Bill is passed in the House of Lords and forwarded for Royal Assent then the Act takes effect on a prescribed day. By convention, the Monarch has no constitutional right not to endorse the Bill.

(2) Amendments are proposed in the Lords. The Bill is sent back to the Commons for consideration before Royal Assent. If no agreement or compromise is reached between the two Houses, the Commons will have the last say.

(3) The House of Lords has no constitutional right to stop a Bill being passed in the elected chamber, the Commons, to become

law by virtue of the Parliament Acts 1911 and 1949. The Act provides that a Bill may be presented for Royal Assent after one year without the agreement from the Lords. For a finance Bill, this time limit is for one month only.

(4) In very exceptional circumstances, usually armed with public support or pure procedural tactics, the House of Lords can delay a Bill, forcing the government to give it up partly or entirely. For example, during the 1997–98 parliamentary session, the Labour government attempted to introduce, as part of a criminal Bill, that the age of consent for homosexuals be reduced. The Lords objected to this and the government were forced to drop this clause, otherwise the enactment of the whole Bill would have been delayed.

Following the adoption of an open government policy by the current Labour Government, Bills are published at the House of Commons website and general public can view any Bills via the internet. Once an Act is enacted, it will also be published in Her Majesty's Stationery Office site at www.hmso.gov.uk/acts

Functions of legislation

Apart from making laws that govern the behaviour of individuals in society, legislation itself possesses the following further specific functions:

- *Revision of substantive rules of law*

  By overruling judicial precedents or repealing previous Acts, expressly or otherwise. When there are two or more conflicting statutes, the latest prevails.

- *Consolidation*

  Previous Acts on a common topic are consolidated in one Act. An example of this is the Company Act 1986, which was consolidated from four previous Acts.

- *Codification*

  Consolidation of rules made by other sources of law. An example is the Sale of Goods Act 1893, which, together with various amendments, was further consolidated into the Sale of Goods Act 1979.

- *Collection of Revenue*

  For example, the Chancellor of Exchequer's Budget.

Supremacy and sovereignty of Parliament

Parliament is said to be supreme. It can make or unmake law created by previous Acts and by the common law system and no court may question the validity of any Act it passes. This is different in some other countries such as the US and Canada, where a court can challenge the legality of a statute on the ground that it is non-constitutional. However, since we joined the European Economic Community, s 2(1) of the European Communities Act 1972 provides that European law created from time to time shall be given effect in UK. In the event of conflict between domestic and European law, the courts must make effective the European law (*Torfaen Borough Council v B&Q* (1990)). Perhaps we can now only say that Parliament is supreme when our law possesses no conflict with the European law. Further, for the purpose of adopting the European Convention on Human Rights into UK law, the Human Rights Act 1998 was enacted. When the Act comes into force in October 2000, judges will have power to make formal declarations where a piece of legislation, past or future, conflicts with the Convention rights. This is not to empower the courts to strike down offending Acts. But, instead, judges are able to declare that the law is incompatible with the Convention, thus prompting Parliament to change it swiftly. In this way, the open ended Convention rights are introduced and will be continuously received into UK law, while the traditional constitutional stance on parliamentary sovereignty is said to have been, to a certain extent, preserved.

Interpretation of statutes

Laws are expressed by words and are, therefore, subject to interpretation as is any form of human expression. Parliament creates statutes and the courts interpret them when they are brought to their attention in cases. When the issues in a statute have been well interpreted in the courts, the statute is said to have been tested and the meaning of it is settled. Throughout the years, the courts have adopted certain rules of interpretation. It should, however, be noted that they are not rules which are only used in the courts. There are similar methods of interpretation that we use in our everyday life.

The Literal Rule
Using the ordinary and natural literal meaning of the words and strictly adhering to them. This is a narrow approach of interpretation

and, by adopting the rule, a statute may produce unworkable or even absurd results. The courts would not intervene but leave it for Parliament to re-enact new law to resolve the problem.

The Golden Rule

Interpreting in a way to avoid absurd results. Section 57 of the Offences Against the Person Act 1861 states that, whosoever being married shall marry any other person, shall be guilty of an offence of bigamy. The defendant in the case of *R v Allan* (1872) used the Literal Rule to argue that, if a person was married, strictly speaking, he could not be married again, therefore, no one could really be guilty under this section. As a judgment, the court interpreted the word in question, 'marry', to mean 'go through the form of marriage', hence avoiding the absurd and unworkable results. The defendant was found guilty. The section was then said to have been tested and the meaning of it was settled.

The Mischief Rule

Interpreting in a way to give effect to the purpose of the legislation. The Street Offences Act 1959 makes it an offence for a common prostitute to loiter or solicit in a street or public place. The defendant in *Smith v Hughes* (1960) only tapped on the first floor window and argued that she was not in the street. Nevertheless, the court held that the purpose of the Act was to clean up the streets and to prevent people from being molested and solicited by common prostitutes and that the defendant was guilty of the offence. This is a wide approach. If the Literal Rule was adopted, the defendant might not have been found guilty.

The *Ejusdem Generis* Rule

'*Ejusdem generis*' means 'of the same kind'. In *Evans v Cross* (1938), a reference in an Act to 'dogs, cats and other animals' was held not to include lions and tigers. 'Other animals' means domestic animals of the same kind as dogs and cats.

The Rule of Exclusion

If the Act says 'dogs and cats', and this is not followed by any general words, it means that the rules apply only to dogs and cats and nothing else.

The *'Noscitur a Sociis'* Rule

Statutes must be read as a whole and the meaning of a word should be comprehended from its context.

Delegated legislation

A vast amount of legislation in this country is made by authorities delegated by Parliament to ministers, government departments, local authorities, nationalised institutions and other public bodies. Such laws are termed 'Statutory Instruments', 'Orders', 'Regulations', 'Bylaws' and 'Orders in Council', etc. These law making powers are usually delegated by Acts of Parliament which are called 'Enabling Acts'.

Forms

- *Order in Council*

  The most dignified form, drafted by a government department for the minister concerned, approved by the Queen in Council (that is, by the Privy Council and signed by the Queen as a formality). Orders in Council are usually used in situations of emergency. For example, the Emergency Powers Act 1920 empowers that regulations can be made by Order in Council for securing the essentials of life to the community following a proclamation of a state of emergency. This could include the use of the armed forces not necessarily to fight but to execute certain tasks.

- *Rule, Regulation, Order, Statutory Instrument and whichever terms are used in the enabling Acts*

  Drafted by a government department for the minister concerned, then laid before Parliament for approval or recognition before or after they come into force. For example, some local authorities make regulations and set levels of fine against dogs fouling in public places. Sometimes, one can find posters or signs stating 'Dog fouling will be prosecuted' or spelling out other local council's regulations on lamp posts and other common areas.

- *Bylaws and Regulations*

  Usually made by local authorities and public bodies such as railway corporations and water authorities; approved by the appropriate government minister. Bylaw posters can be seen at many main railway and underground stations.

One must not have the impression that delegated legislation is a subordinate source of legislation and, therefore, is not as important as statutes made by Parliament. The laws and rules made under delegated legislation are as equally enforceable as any Acts of Parliament. A person can be prosecuted for misconduct in a railway station or carriage in a criminal court in the same way as for any other criminal offences.

Criticism and justification

Criticism

A matter of principle
It is said that by delegated legislation we have given law making powers to those who are not elected by us, hence, falling foul of the democratic principle.

Inadequate publicity
There are over 2,000 statutory instruments made each year and many are inadequately publicised. An ordinary citizen cannot be expected to know all of these changes every year to keep on the right side of the law. This raises the question of whether the principle 'ignorance of the law is no excuse' should hold. For delegated legislation to exist, there must be good justification and control must be adequate.

Justification

Lack of parliamentary time
Each year, there are about 60 Acts passed in Parliament and there are over 2,000 pieces of delegated legislation issued. It is impossible for Parliament to deal with every minor detail of law.

Technicality of the subject matter
An enabling Act is sometimes described as a 'skeleton' which spells out the principle of the law. Technical and sometimes complex details, for example, building regulations and regulations relating to medicine and drugs are left to administrators, who are often more familiar with the subject than most MPs.

Flexibility and future needs
Parliament may anticipate possible growth in the subject matter and some practical difficulties in implementing the law, but it does not always know exactly what they are. Therefore, some details and room for future additions are left to those who administer the law. By using statutory instruments, administrators can add and amend necessary details efficiently. Further, when a piece of law becomes obsolete,

unfair or unworkable, statutory instrument can change the problem situation much quicker than the more rigid parliamentary legislation. An Act is still the law unless it is repealed by another statute and the enactment can be a long process, especially to those who are affected by an obsolete law.

Urgency

Parliament is not always in session and, even when it is, legislative procedures are slow. In the event of an emergency, delegated legislation is the best means of dealing with the situation quickly.

Locality

Local knowledge is sometimes required when rules and bylaws are needed for a particular area. The details of such rules are left to the local administrators. Common examples of this are regulations concerning parking control in a particular district, including parking tariffs and levels of fine against illegal parking. Next time you see a parking ticket, try to identify the enabling Act and the name of the local regulation.

Control of delegated legislation

By Parliament

- Many enabling Acts contain certain provisions requiring delegated legislation to be laid before Parliament. This is a means for Parliament to retain its right to inspect, approve or disapprove laws which are made under the delegated authority.

- The Joint Committee on Statutory Instruments was set up in 1974. Its role is to scrutinise and, when appropriate, draw the House's attention to certain rules and regulations made. It also has the power to demand an explanation from relevant government departments.

- The responsible minister may be questioned during the House of Commons' Question Time on matters relating to law made by delegated legislation.

- Law making powers are granted by Parliament, which can also revoke and vary the delegated power by passing another Act. This is the ultimate control.

By the courts

There are three main grounds on which a court can challenge a piece of statutory instrument.

- *Ultra vires*

  A court can hold that an instrument has been made *ultra vires*, that is, 'beyond the power'. This means that the relevant law making authority has exceeded the power conferred to it by the enabling Act. In *Bromley London Borough Council v Greater London Council* (1982), the GLC Transport (London) Act 1969 provides that the GLC had a general duty to provide an integrated, efficient and economic transport system for the Greater London area. The GLC reduced fares by 25% and required London boroughs to increase rates to pay for the cost. Bromley LBC claimed that the GLC had acted beyond their lawful power and the House of Lords agreed. The policy was held void.

- *Unreasonableness*

  In *Kruse v Johnson* (1898), Lord Russell set out that, if rules are manifestly unjust, if they disclose bad faith, or if they involve:

  ... such oppressive or gratuitous interference with the rights of those subject to them as can find no justification in the minds of reasonable men, the court might well say Parliament never intended to give authority to make such rules; they are unreasonable and *ultra vires*.

- *Contrary to European law*

  R v Secretary of State of Social Security ex p Joint Council for the Welfare of Immigrants (1996) was a judicial review case examining regulations made by the Secretary of State to exclude immigrants from claiming State benefits. It was held that any delegated legislation which exclude, *inter alia*, treaties and conventions ratified here and in the European Union are invalid, therefore, the regulations in question were unlawful.

Other controls

- *Consultation*

  Some enabling Acts set out that the Minister concerned must consult certain advisory bodies or submit drafts of the proposed instruments for their approvals. In practice, Ministers often consult experts and take advice from organisations which will likely be affected by proposed legislation. For example, before road traffic legislation is proposed, organisations such as the Automobile Association (AA), RAC, motor manufacturers or their associations may be consulted.

- *Publication*

  Her Majesty's Stationery Office (HMSO) publishes lists showing dates of issue of statutory instruments. The Statutory Instruments Act 1946 provides that:

  ... it shall be a defence to prove that the instrument had not been issued by HMSO at the date of the alleged contravention, unless it is proved that, at that date, reasonable steps had been taken for the purpose of bringing the purport of the instrument to the notice of the public, or of the persons likely to be affected by it, or of the person charged.

Common law system

A good legal system should be consistent, yet, when necessary, be flexible enough to allow changes. Amongst other advantages, the common law system has helped to achieve these objectives in many ways. These are outlined below.

Doctrine of judicial precedent

The basis of the common law system is the doctrine of judicial precedent, which governs that judges, when making their judgments in court, are bound to follow the legal principle laid down by other judges in earlier cases decided in courts of same and higher standings. The building blocks of the doctrine are law reports. If a legal principle has to be referred to in future cases, they have to be recorded accurately. There are many law reports, some recording significant cases in general, for example, the All England Law Reports (All ER) and the Times Law Reports (TLR) and some reporting particular areas of law, for example, Tax Cases (TC). Since November 1996, all official reports of cases are published at the House of Lords and the Court of Appeal websites within two hours of delivery there. A case report normally contains (a) the finding of facts; (b) statements of principle of law applying to the facts, this is called the *ratio decidendi*; and (c) the decision, that is, A wins B loses. For the purpose of the doctrine of precedent, the *ratio decidendi* is the vital element. It can be defined as the statement of law applied to the legal problem raised by the facts as found upon which the decision is based. It is the *ratio decidendi* which forms a precedent and binds future cases.

Obiter dicta

Judgments sometimes contain additional statements of law which are known as *obiter dicta*. These Latin words mean 'something said by the way'. There are two types of *obiter dicta*:

- A statement based upon facts which were not found to exist. For example, a judge may say 'If A did otherwise, I would have made a different decision'. By saying this, the judge has expressed another set of legal principles which he would apply on the 'otherwise' situation.
- A statement based on facts found. However, this does not form the basis of the decision, for example, a dissenting (minority) judgment.

Obiter dicta are not binding precedents, but they do have persuasive effects and sometimes judges refer to them.

Stare decisis

The principle which underpins the approach under the common law system is called *stare decisis* which means 'standing of decision'. Not all judges' decisions create binding precedents and some courts are more important than others. The general rules are that lower courts are bound by decisions of higher courts and some courts are bound by their own previous decisions.

Further details regarding the hierarchy and standing of the courts are as follows:

- *House of Lords*

  Is the final court of appeal on points of law for the whole of the UK in civil cases and for England, Wales and Northern Ireland in criminal cases. Decisions in the House bind all courts in England and Wales. Since Lord Gardiner's Practice Statement issued in 1966, the House needs not follow its own past decisions, hence allowing some room for law to change and to grow.

- *Court of Appeal (Civil Division)*

  Is bound by the House of Lords' decisions. The case of *Young v Bristol Aeroplane Company* (1978) laid down the principle that the

Court of Appeal is bound by its own previous decisions except in the cases where:

- ○ the previous decision was *per incuriam* (in error);
- ○ there are two previous conflicting decisions of the 'Court of Appeal which a judge may then choose between; or
- ○ the previous decision conflicts with a later House of Lords' judgment.

- *Court of Appeal (Criminal Division)*

  The position is the same as in the Civil Division except that a judge can rely on a further ground not to follow the Court of Appeal's previous decisions, namely, that it would cause injustice to the appellant.

- *Queen's Bench Divisional Court*

  Deals with criminal cases appealed to it from the Crown Court and the magistrates' courts by way of case stated, that is, when the party only appeals against the application of the law, but not against the facts found. Its decisions bind the magistrates' courts but not the Crown Court and the court normally follows its own decisions.

- *High Court*

  Its decisions bind county courts but not itself, though they may be persuasive.

Decisions in the Crown Court, county courts and magistrates' courts do not form any precedent and, therefore, bind no one.

Other concepts

- *Distinguishing*

  Although the facts of a case appear to be similar to those of a binding precedent, a judge may consider that there are some aspects or facts which are not covered by the *ratio decidendi* of the earlier case. Based on this, the judge may *distinguish* his case from the previous case and decide not to follow the precedent.

- *Reversing*

  If an appeal court comes to the same decision as the court below, it is said to have upheld that decision. If it decides the other way, it is said to have *reversed* the decision of the court below.

- *Overruling*

  If a court in a *later case* is faced with an earlier decision of a *lower court*, or a court of the same standing, it may follow that *ratio decidendi* or consider it incorrect. If it does the latter, then the earlier decision is said to be *overruled*.

- *Disapproval*

  Although a *ratio* is followed, a superior court may consider that there is some doubt as to the standing of the principle and it may *disapprove* it using *obiter dicta*, but not expressly overrule the earlier precedent.

Advantages

- *Certainty*

  In a court case, the decision does not totally depend on one or two persons' judgment (that is, by the judge at the time) or arguments by the lawyer. Judgments have to be supported by legal principle and authorities, which are recorded black and white in law reports. Interpretations of Acts of Parliament are tested by actual cases. Once a precedent is set, it will be followed by future cases.

- *Detailed and practical*

  Legal principle based on real facts, not just words.

- *Provision for growth*

  Acts of Parliament cannot cover all situations and judges can make decisions in almost all circumstances when they are brought in front of them, therefore, it is possible for judges, especially those in higher courts, to create legal principle when appropriate. This is further enhanced by the fact that now the House of Lords is not strictly bound by its own previous decisions.

Disadvantages

- *Rigidity*

  When a bad decision is set, or a *ratio* becomes obsolete, it takes time and resources to overrule it. Before it is overruled, the legal principle remains the law of the land. In other countries which do not practice common law, judges have more discretion not to follow previous decisions against obsolete law or when doing so will result in hardship or unjust situations.

21

- *Danger of illogical distinctions*

  Sometimes, in order to avoid following a rule which may result in an unjust situation, a judge may lay hold of minute distinctions from the main line of law. Some writers argue that this allows the law to grow and to cover various circumstances but some others would comment that this leads to confusion.

- *Complexity and large volume of law reports*

European Community law (of the European Union)

Background

Following the signing of three major European Communities treaties and the passage of the European Communities Act 1972, the UK became a member of the European Economic Community on 1 January 1973. A referendum was held in 1975, where it was decided, by a 2:1 majority, that we would stay in the Community. Section 2(1) of the 1972 Act provides that law, from time to time created or arising by or under the treaties, are without further enactment to be given legal effect or used in the UK.

Organisation

- *Commission*

  There are 15 Member States. France, Italy, UK, Spain and Germany have two commissioners and others have one commissioner each. The function of the Commission is to make sure that the treaties are upheld. It also initiates legislation to the Council. It is not the major law making body, but has some legislative power in certain detailed regulations.

- *Council of Ministers*

  This is the primary legislative organisation. It is made up of 15 senior ministers from the Member States.

- *Parliament*

  Again, this is not the primary law making institute, but a consultative one. One of its major functions is the control of budgets.

- *Court of Justice*

  Article 234 of the Treaty of Amsterdam 1997 allows a Member State to refer issues of Community law to the European Court of Justice for a ruling which binds the Member State in question.

Forms of Community legislation

- *Regulations*

  Bind Member States without reference to any of their domestic law making bodies.

- *Decisions*

  Rules particularly addressed to a single State or an individual (or individual corporation).

- *Directives*

  Bind all Member States, but the States must bring it into being by whatever means. In the UK, this can be achieved by statutory instrument or by passing an Act. Usually, a time limit for implementation of the law is imposed by the Directive. The Commercial Agents (Council Directive) Regulation 1993 came into force on 1 January 1994, making effective a 1986 Directive. The Regulations unify relationships of commercial agents with their principals and they offer greater protection to agents within the European Union. The Trade Mark Act 1993 was made law on 31 October 1994, making effective a 1989 Directive which harmonises trade mark law within the Union.

Effects of European Union law on the English courts

- Individuals can sue and take legal action in an English court based on European law.
- Section 3(1) of the 1972 Act provides that questions as to the validity, meaning or effect of Community law shall be determined in the courts of the UK in accordance with the principles laid down by the European Court.
- Further, the courts can request an interpretation of a European law from the European Court of Justice. Decisions from the European Court must be accepted.

- Regarding the effect on binding precedent, in the event of a conflict between domestic law and the European law, the latter prevails.

The European Convention on Human Rights and Fundamental Freedoms 1950

The UK has been a member of the European Convention on Human Rights and Fundamental Freedoms 1950 for 50 years, but no law has been enacted to adopt the Convention until the Human Rights Act 1998, which will be fully implemented on 2 October 2000. One must note that the Convention mainly deals with human rights and fundamental freedom issues, and it is separate to the European Union.

The 1998 Act, among other things, provides that:

- individuals can bring a case regarding the Convention rights in the UK domestic courts;
- courts or tribunals, when determining questions that have arisen in connection with the Convention rights, must take into account any judgments, decision, declarations or advisory opinions of the European Court of Human Rights and other formal opinions and decisions arising from the Convention;
- legislation must be read and given effect in a way that is compatible with the Convention rights;
- judges will have power to make formal declarations where UK laws conflict with the Convention rights.

3 Criminal Law

You should be familiar with the following areas:

- various elements in crime
- *mens rea, actus reus* and strict liability
- minors in criminal law
- definition and specific defences of murder
- different forms of manslaughter
- definitions and requirements of various assault offences
- definitions and requirements of theft and other offences against property
- various general defences and their applications

Nature of criminal liability

What is crime?

Halsbury's Laws of England defines crime as:

> ... an unlawful act or default which is an offence against the public and renders the person guilty of the act or default liable to legal punishment.

Two main objectives of criminal law are:

(a)   to punish and reform the offenders; and

(b)   to protect the public and individuals from harm which may be caused by the unlawful act or default.

Classification of crime

The following are three main ways that various offences can be classified:

Classification by the method of trial

There are summary, indictable and either way offences. Summary offences are those which are triable in magistrates' courts only and heard by magistrates. They are usually less serious crimes. Indictable offences are those which can only be tried in the Crown Court, heard by a judge and a jury. The judge deals with issues of law and the jury decides on facts. There are also either-way offences, which can be tried either in magistrates' courts or the Crown Court. All criminal cases start in magistrates' courts; therefore, if a case is an either way offence or an indictable offence, there are procedures to decide in which court the matter is to be heard and to transfer the case to the Crown Court. Further details of these procedures are stated in Chapter 9.

Statutory and common law offences

Statutory offences are those crimes that are provided by Acts of Parliament or by delegated legislation. The Act or the regulation normally provides a statutory definition for the offence. All the elements stated in the definition have to be proven before an accused can be convicted. Examples include various offences against property such as theft, robbery, burglary and many others that are provided in the Theft Act 1968 and the Theft Act 1978. Common law offences are those which were created by the common law system, for example, murder. Some crimes can be statutory as well as common law offences, for example, assault and battery. The Offences Against the Person Act 1861 has defined several assault related offences providing different maximum penalties according to the seriousness of the offence. The Act, however, has not abolished the common law assault and battery, which therefore have survived the statute.

Classification by the power of arrest

The Police and Criminal Evidence Act 1984 provides that certain types of offences are arrestable offences and the same Act confers power to police officers to arrest a person without a warrant if they have reasonable grounds to suspect a person has committed, is committing or is about to commit such an offence. Other offences should be described as 'an offence which is not an arrestable offence'. There is no such thing as a non-arrestable offence because, for an offence which is not an arrestable offence, a police officer can still arrest in the same way as for an arrestable offence if certain further conditions are satisfied. More details regarding arrestable offences are explained in Chapter 9.

Elements of crime

Generally, a crime should consist of two main components, that is, a guilty act (*actus reus*) and a guilty mind (*mens rea*). In other words, the accused should not be convicted if the prosecution fails to prove either of these components. Further, a crime may require more than one *actus reus* or *mens rea*. For the prosecution to be successful, all the external and mental elements must be proven.

Actus reus

Actus reus refers to the external elements of a crime and includes all those parts of an offence, except those which relate to the accused's state of mind. This is not restricted to an act. It can be the circumstances in which the act occurs, a condition, a state of affairs, a consequence or even an omission. Section 1 of the Theft Act 1968 defines that theft is committed when a person dishonestly appropriates property belonging to another with the intention to permanently deprive the other of it. The dishonesty and the intention to permanently deprive are the mental elements and are, therefore, the *mens rea* of the offence. The appropriation is an act and is, therefore, an *actus reus*. An accused may argue that the property belongs to him and, therefore, the circumstance that it actually belongs to another has to be proven to convict. Murder is the unlawful killing of another under the Queen's peace with malice aforethought. The act of killing is an *actus reus*. The required circumstances of unlawfulness and of 'under the Queen's peace' have nothing to do with the accused's state of mind and are, therefore, also part of the *actus reus*. When a soldier kills during wartime, it is generally lawful. Malice aforethought, which means intention to kill or to cause grievous bodily harm, is the *mens rea* of murder. There used to be a further requirement that the death must occur within a year and one day. This describes a consequence of the guilty act and is, therefore, also an *actus reus*. The Law Reform (Year and Day Rule) Act 1996 has, however, abolished this requirement. In *R v Larsonneur* (1933), the defendant was convicted of being found in the UK without having leave (that is, permission) to enter, despite the fact that she had been forcibly brought into the jurisdiction in the custody of the Irish Free State police. The case set out the rule that it is not necessary for the prosecution to prove that the defendant caused the state of affairs.

Generally, omission cannot give rise to criminal liability except in some specific situations. In *R v Miller* (1983), the defendant was squatting in a house and fell asleep holding a cigarette. He awoke and found that the mattress was smouldering, but he simply moved to another room to continue his sleep. The House of Lords held that, although the defendant created a dangerous situation accidentally, he made no attempt to mitigate the damage. In the circumstances, he was under a duty to act and failure to do so gave rise to criminal liability. Other duties of this nature can arise from statute, such as certain parental, family and contractual relationships.

Mens rea

Mens rea refers to the mental elements of a crime or the offender's state of mind when the crime is being committed. This can be intention, recklessness or gross negligence.

Intention

There are direct and indirect (or oblique) intentions. Direct intention occurs when a person desires an event and his purpose is to cause that event. It is not as straight forward for indirect intention. It may be apparent that an offender brought about the *actus reus* of a crime, but he could argue that he did not intend to cause that particular outcome. For example, if a terrorist leaves a bomb at a station and A is killed by the explosion, the terrorist may say that he had no direct intention to kill A in particular, thus he had not committed murder.

In *R v Steane* (1947), a narrow approach was adopted. Steane was charged with intentionally assisting the enemy by giving broadcasts for the Nazis during the war. The court found in his favour stating that he did not intend to assist the enemy but only intended to avoid the concentration camp. In *Hyam v DPP* (1974), the court found that the defendant only intended to make a threat by putting a blazing newspaper through the letterbox of a house in the middle of the night. As a consequence, the house was burnt and two children were killed. The House of Lords held that Hyam was guilty of murder since she knew that it was highly likely that her act would cause at least serious bodily harm. It did not matter whether she actually intended the consequence or not and the indirect intention was sufficient. This wide approach, in a way equating intention with foresight, was later silently overruled. In *R v Moloney* (1985), Moloney fired a gun in a family party during a friendly challenge of who could draw the gun quickest. As a result, he killed his stepfather. The House of Lords reduced his murder conviction to manslaughter. In *R v Hancock and Shankland* (1986), two miners threw a block of concrete over a bridge intending to block the road but a taxi driver was killed. The House of Lords held that it was wrong for the trial judge to direct the jury to apply a test of 'natural consequence' to decide whether there was an intention to kill or cause serious bodily harm. As a result, the conviction was again reduced to manslaughter. In both *Moloney* and *Hancock and Shankland*, the House of Lords set out the principle that a trial judge should avoid any elaboration or paraphrase of what is meant by intention and should leave it to the jury to decide on the issue. Only when it is absolutely necessary in difficult cases and to avoid misunderstanding, a judge may give an explanation on what intention means using the concept of probability. In *Hancock and Shankland*, the elaboration in the House of Lords was that foresight of consequence was not the same as intention but of evidence of circumstances. The greater the probability of the consequence, the more likely it was foreseen and, hence, the more likely it was intended. There is, however, no fixed formula on the words to be used for the explanation and it would depend on the individual case. In *R v Nedrick* (1986), it was said that the jury were not entitled to infer the necessary intention, unless they felt sure that death or serious bodily harm was a virtually certain result of the defendant's action and he appreciated that. In *R v Walker and Hayles* (1990), the words 'very high degree of probability of death' were used.

It is still not absolutely clear, especially in some complicated cases, what is meant by intention. It is, however, clear that a person can be convicted on direct or oblique intention. To go back to the original example of a terrorist leaving a bomb at a station, the court may find no necessity to elaborate to the jury on the meaning of intent and the jury may have no difficulty in coming to a conclusion that there was an intention to kill or to cause grievous bodily harm. It may not be as straightforward if the terrorist has given detailed warning and taken some specific precautions then the judge may have to deliver some explanation to the jury. If he does, he should do so according to the guidelines laid down in *Moloney*, *Hancock*, *Nedrick* and *Walker*.

Recklessness

There are also two types of recklessness. The first is often called *Cunningham* recklessness after the case of *R v Cunningham* (1957). This is the traditional meaning of recklessness, which occurs when a person has recognised a risk, but has decided to ignore it while a reasonable person would not. The other type of recklessness occurs when a person has not given any thought of or has failed to realise the risk, which a prudent bystander would realise and would not take such a risk. This is often referred to as *Caldwell* recklessness after *R v Caldwell* (1981). The major distinction between recklessness and intention is that there is no desire to cause the event in recklessness. The main difference between the two types of recklessness is that there is awareness of the risk in *Cunningham*, but not in *Caldwell*. Lord Diplock in *Caldwell* argued that a person who fails to give any thought to an obvious risk is just as dangerous as the person who realises the risk.

Since *Caldwell*, the new approach was accepted in many cases until cases such as *Elliot v C* (1983), which received much criticism. In the case, an educationally sub-normal 14 year old girl was convicted of criminal damage for setting fire to a shed. She was guilty of failing to appreciate a risk which a reasonable person would have appreciated. The main argument against *Caldwell* is that it criminalises people who are not capable of meeting the standards of a reasonable person. In view of the above, the courts have recently retreated from *Caldwell* when dealing with the issue regarding which type of recklessness applies depending on the individual offence. For example:

- for indecent assault, the courts would require that the defendant must be aware of the risk;
- for rape, the defendant must be indifferent or couldn't care less whether the woman consented to sexual intercourse. This is somewhere in between *Cunningham* and *Caldwell*;
- in *R v Savage* (1991), the House of Lords confirmed that *Cunningham* should be applied to all non-fatal offences against the person when recklessness is an issue.

Negligence
Negligence describes a state of mind when an accused's conduct fails to measure up to the conduct of a reasonable person. It does not require desire, foresight or awareness. Examples of crimes which only require negligence as *mens rea* include:

- dangerous driving and causing death by dangerous driving as provided in s 1 of the Road Traffic Act 1991, amending the Road Traffic Act 1988, replacing the two similar reckless driving offences which required recklessness;
- manslaughter, which can be committed by grossly negligent conduct.

Strict liability

These are crimes for which *mens rea* is not essential. This may be described as an exception to the general rule that a crime requires both *actus reus* and *mens rea*. They are usually statutory offences created for one of the following three main purposes:

- *Petty offences*

  These are very minor offences and it is not worth the courts' while or even the offenders' to spend time and effort to prove or disprove *mens rea*. Good examples of this are motoring and parking offences.

- *Protection of the public*

  Sometimes, this can be regarded as social legislation. The general principle is that a person should not be guilty of a crime if he is not at fault or he did not have the appropriate guilty mind. However, there are situations and activities which can be so hazardous and dangerous that Parliament would sacrifice the above principle for the purpose of protecting the public or preventing the situation from happening in the first place. Examples of these include the Health and Safety at Work, etc, Act (for example, it is an offence not to install safety covers for certain hazardous machinery); the Consumer Protection Act 1987; the Pollution Act; some food and hygiene legislation to ensure that food sold to the public is fit for consumption; and some offence relating to controlled drugs.

- *Promotion of fair trading*

  These are regulations to promote fair trading, in breach of which is a criminal offence. A good example of this is various labelling regulations which help consumers to make informed choices, require warnings to be given in tobacco or other hazardous products as well as helping to promote fair trading practice.

When a statute does not state clearly that an offence is one of strict liability, the courts tend to require proof of fault (*Sherras v De Rutzen* (1895)), in particular, when an offence is a serious one. In *Sweet v Parsley* (1970), the defendant was originally convicted for being concerned in the management of premises which were used for the purpose of smoking cannabis, contrary to s 5(1)(b) of the Dangerous Drugs Act 1965, although she only visited the premises to collect rent and did not know it was used for that purpose. The House of Lords quashed her conviction, confirming the above principle.

Minors in criminal law

A child under 10 years of age is irrebuttably presumed to be legally incapable of committing a crime, however, he may be subject to care proceedings. A boy under 14 years old is irrebuttably presumed to be legally incapable of committing a crime of which sexual intercourse is an element, for example, rape. 'Young persons', that is, those aged 17 and younger, are fully liable to any crime, the same way as adults, but their cases are dealt with in the youth court. Details regarding the youth court will be discussed in Chapter 9.

Other aspects

Conspiracy

Section 1(1) of the Criminal Law Act 1977, as amended by s 5 of the Criminal Attempts Act 1981, provides that, if a person agrees with any other person or persons that a course of conduct shall be pursued which, if the agreement is carried out in accordance with their intentions, either:

(a) will necessarily amount to or involve the commission of any offence or offences by one or more of the parties to the agreement; or

(b) would do so but for the existence of facts which render the commission of the offence or any of the offences impossible,

he is guilty of conspiracy to commit the offence of offences in question.

Aiding and abetting

Two or more persons can be charged as joint principal defendants. Further, a person who aids, abets, counsels or procures the commission of the *actus reus* by a principal can be charged as a secondary offender. A secondary offender is liable to be tried, indicted and punished as a principal offender (s 8 of the Accessories and Abettors Act 1861, as amended by s 12 of the Criminal Law Act 1977).

Attempt

Section 1(1) of the Criminal Attempts Act 1981 provides that it is an offence for a person, with intent to commit an offence to which s 1 applies, to do an act which is more than merely preparatory to the commission of the offence. By s 1(4), the following crimes cannot be attempted:

- summary offences;
- conspiracy;
- aiding, abetting, counselling or procuring an offence; and
- assisting an offender or concealing an offence contrary to ss 4 and 5 of the Criminal Law Act 1967.

Offences against the person

These include fatal offences such as murder and manslaughter and non-fatal ones like assault and battery.

Murder

Murder is a common law offence which can be defined as the unlawful killing of another human being with malice aforethought. The killing must be unlawful and, therefore, killing an enemy during wartime may be lawful. The attack must lead to a killing so it must cause the death. In *R v Jordan* (1956), the court held that gross negligent medical treatment after an attack was the actual cause of the death and, therefore, Jordan was acquitted for murder. In a later case of *R v Smith* (1959), it was held that negligent, as opposed to grossly negligent, medical treatment will not break the chain of causation and Smith was convicted of murder. When it was difficult in the past to prove causation after a long period of time had passed from an attack to the death, it was the law that the death must occur within one year and a day. With the advancement of medical science, the Law Reform (Year and a Day Rule) Act 1996 abolished the rule. The victim must be another human being. A person killing himself is suicide, which is not a crime. However, it is a criminal offence to aid, abet, counsel or procure the suicide of another as provided by the Suicide Act 1961. The cases discussed above are the *actus reus* of murder. The *mens rea* is malice aforethought which means an intention to kill or cause grievous bodily harm. If a person does not intend to kill, but only intends to cause serious bodily harm, and the victim dies, the attacker can still be convicted for murder.

The punishment for murder is imprisonment for life. Sometimes, it is described as a crime with punishment fixed by the law. In practice, a convicted murderer can be released from prison on licence and the trial judge may recommend to the Home Secretary a minimum term to be served before any release may take place.

Specific defences for murder

Other general defences may help the accused. The following two specific defences are only available for murder.

Diminished responsibility

Section 2 of the Homicide Act 1957 provides that an accused shall not be convicted of murder if he can show that he was suffering from an abnormality of the mind at the time of the killing. The scope of abnormality of the mind is very wide; the section further provides that it can arise from a condition of arrested or retarded development of mind or any inherent causes or induced by disease or injury. As long as it has substantially impaired the accused's mental responsibility for his acts or omissions which cause the death, it will be sufficient. On this basis, the jury may reduce the conviction to manslaughter.

Provocation

As for diminished responsibility, if provocation is successfully pleaded, a conviction will be reduced to manslaughter. The accused must show:

- The action and behaviour of the provoker would make any reasonable person lose control of their mind. In *DPP v Camplin* (1978), the House of Lords explained what it means by 'reasonable person' who is a person sharing the accused's characteristics relevant to the case. Section 3 of the Homicide Act 1957 clarifies that provocation can be 'things said' as well as 'things done'. In *R v Davies* (1975), it was held that provocation does not have to come from the victim.

- The loss of self-control was sudden and temporary at the time of the killing, as held in the case of *R v Duffy* (1949).

Provocation in the context of battered woman syndrome

Due to the increase in domestic violence against women, the courts have recently been re-examining the law relating to provocation, which requires sudden and temporary loss of self-control, in the context of battered woman syndrome.

Many writers comment that the law of provocation treats women unfairly because they are often temperamentally different from men and not as physically strong as their partners. Victims of domestic violence often would not and could not defend themselves or react spontaneously. However, their emotions and feelings can be so suppressed that this may lead them to kill their abusers when they are in a more vulnerable state, for example, sleeping or drunk. Previous cases have failed to address such a deeply affected state of mind until recently in the two very similar cases of *Ahluwalia* and *Thornton*. Mrs Ahluwalia suffered many years of physical and sexual abuse from her husband. One day in March 1989, her husband left home for a few days. On his return, he started threatening her again and Mrs Ahluwalia, who had purchased a can of petrol with a view to using it on her husband, waited until he was asleep and poured it over him. She lit it and he died from burns some days later. At Mrs Ahluwalia's trial, provocation was pleaded and the judge directed the jury that the defence was available only if she suffered a sudden and temporary loss of self-control. She was convicted of murder. She appealed on the grounds that the judge had misdirected the jury and that there was fresh evidence of her diminished responsibility which had not been put forward at the trial. The appeal failed on the grounds of provocation, but succeeded in relation to diminished responsibility. The conviction was set aside and a retrial was ordered. At the retrial, a manslaughter plea was accepted and the defendant was sentenced to 40 months imprisonment which she had served exactly.

In *R v Thornton* (1992), Mrs Thornton also suffered from domestic violence from her husband. In the last incident, she went into the kitchen, calmed herself down, then looked for a weapon, sharpened a carving knife, went back to the living room and killed her husband. The original trial held again that there was no sudden loss of self-control and she was convicted of murder. On appeal, the Court of Appeal confirmed the conviction. In 1995, after tireless campaigning by some women's welfare groups, the Home Secretary referred the case back to the Court of Appeal pursuant to the Criminal Appeal Act 1968. The basis was that there was new evidence showing the accused's personality disorder at the time and the effects of the husband's abuse over a period of time on her mental state. The court was asked to consider whether a reasonable woman with the characteristics of a 'battered woman' might have lost her self-control and killed her husband. The case also re-examined whether the loss of control had to be sudden and temporary, which the Court affirmed. Based on the new evidence provided, the court ordered a retrial and it was retried in May 1998 in Oxford Crown Court. Mrs Thornton was convicted of manslaughter and sentenced to five years' imprisonment, which she had already served.

In the light of these cases, it may be concluded that the court is reluctant to change the legal principle regarding provocation. The courts do not want to widen the scope of provocation as a defence for murder. On the other hand, it appears that the courts are prepared to put 'battered woman syndrome' into the equation when considering provocation and to accept diminished responsibility when proven.

Manslaughter

There are three situations in which manslaughter can occur. We have discussed the first situation when a person has successfully pleaded provocation or diminished responsibility. Further, when two or more persons agree that they shall be killed by some means, this is what is called a suicide pact. Successful pleas of provocation, diminished responsibility and suicide pact will reduce a murder conviction to manslaughter and they are classified as voluntary manslaughter. The other two situations are what is called 'involuntary manslaughter', which occur when a person has:

(a)   unlawfully killed with gross negligence; or

(b)   intentionally committed a dangerous criminal act which resulted in the death of the victim.

The latter includes the situation when a victim is killed by a third party, for example, by using a victim as a shield when shooting at the police.

The maximum punishment for manslaughter is life imprisonment.

Causing death by dangerous driving

The offence of causing death by dangerous driving, as provided by ss 1 and 2A of the Road Traffic Act 1988, has replaced the previous crime of causing death by reckless driving. The dangerous driving offence uses the gross negligence test while the old reckless driving offence required the *Caldwell* objective recklessness. The maximum sentence is five years' imprisonment.

Common law assault and battery

Assault and battery are common law offences which create civil as well as criminal liabilities. Assault is intentionally, or recklessly, causing another person to apprehend immediate and unlawful personal violence (*Fagan v Metropolitan Police Commissioner* (1968)). It does not require any contact between the parties; a threatening gesture is sufficient. Generally, there has to be some form of action. Words alone, however insulting, are generally not classed as common assault.

Battery is 'intentionally or recklessly applying unlawful physical force or violence to another person'. Assault and battery, by their legal meanings, are two different things. Therefore, attack from behind is only battery, but not assault. However, in practice, the word 'assault' is often used to include battery, even in statutes, and students must not be confused by this. Specific defences against a charge can include consent, self-defence, parental and guardian parental authority (that is, parents and teachers disciplining their children and students).

Some statutory offences relating to assault and battery under the Offences Against the Person Act 1861

Section 47 offence: Assault occasioning (means causing) actual bodily harm

Actual bodily harm (ABH) is generally taken as any hurt or injury which interferes with the health and comfort of the victim. In practice, s 47 offence lies somewhere between common assault and a serious wounding which requires breaking of the skin. Examples of ABH include loss of a tooth or teeth, bruises, broken nose, minor fractures, and minor cuts of a sort probably requiring medical treatment (for example, stitches). It was confirmed in *R v Chan-Fook* (1993) that ABH includes psychiatric injury but not emotional impact such as fear, distress or panic. In *R v Ireland* (1997), the defendant made nuisance telephone calls remaining silent during the calls to his victim. It was established that psychiatric harm comes within the scope of ABH even possibly grievous bodily harm in ss 18 and 20). The common law principle that words alone are not sufficient does not apply to these statutory offences. The maximum penalty is five years' imprisonment.

Section 18 offence

Whosoever shall *unlawfully and maliciously* by any means whatsoever *wound or cause any grievous bodily harm* (GBH) to any person: (1) *with intent to cause GBH* to any person; or (2) *with intent to resist or prevent the lawful apprehension* or detainer of any person.

In short, it is the unlawful and malicious wounding or causing GBH to another person with intent to harm or prevent arrest. There are two offences, that is, wounding or causing GBH. Wounding requires breaking of the skin, therefore, in the case of internal haemorrhage, burns or broken bones the charge should be GBH. GBH simply means serious bodily harm. The maximum penalty is life imprisonment.

Section 20 offence

Similar to s 18, but there is no need to show intent. Maximum penalty is five years' imprisonment. In *R v Burstow* (1996), a stalker was held to have inflicted harm contrary to s 20 in the absence of a direct assault. It has been commented that using these statutory offences against stalking is far from satisfactory because these offenders mainly cause psychiatric harm to their victims and such harm may not be serious enough to warrant a conviction. Even if it does, it has to be proven by appropriate psychiatric expert evidence, which is not as easily established as for other injuries. This brought about the introduction of the anti-stalking law, the Protection from Harassment Act 1997, which covers a wide scope of harassment situations including racial harassment. The maximum penalty for this offence is five years' imprisonment.

Other examples of offences against a person

- *Racially aggravated assaults*

  For the above assault offences, if racially aggravated, they carry higher penalties.

- *Section 38 of the 1861 Act*

  Assault intending to resist arrest.

- *Section 51(1) of the Police Act 1964*

  Assault a constable during the execution of his duty.

- *Section 1 of the Sexual Offences Act 1956*

  Rape is the unlawful sexual intercourse with a woman without her free consent. *R v R* (1991) confirmed, for the first time, that a husband can be convicted of raping his wife. Indecent assault on a woman is an offence under s 14 and on a man is an offence under s 15 of the 1956 Act.

  The Criminal Justice and Public Order Act 1994 created the offence of male rape with a maximum life sentence. The effect of the Act is to extend the definition of rape to include all acts of non-consensual intercourse against men and women.

Offences against property

Theft

By s 1(1) of the Theft Act 1968:

> ... a person is guilty of theft if he dishonestly appropriates property belonging to another with the intention of permanently depriving the other of it.

All of the following five elements have to be proven to secure a conviction:

- *Actus reus*

  'Appropriation', 'property' and 'belonging to another'.

- *Mens rea*

  'Dishonesty' and 'intention to permanently deprive'.

The maximum penalty for theft is 10 years' imprisonment.

Appropriation

Appropriation does not only mean taking, procuring, obtaining and the like. Section 3(1) of the 1968 Act provides that appropriation has taken place when a person assumes or takes over the right of an owner. In *R v Morris* (1983), the defendant substituted a lower priced label on an article displayed in a supermarket. He had no right to do this and by doing so he had assumed the right of an owner.

Property

Section 4(1) of the 1968 Act defines property as money and all other property, real or personal, including things in action and other intangible property. Things in action are legal rights such as debt and other liabilities. Similar to other intangible properties like copyright, patents and shares. It may be difficult to appreciate how these things can be stolen. The simple answer is that they may be appropriated by any assumption of the rights of the owner. Other sub-sections in s 4 provide that wild plants cannot be stolen, unless they are picked for reward or sale. Section 4(4) provides that an animal in the wild, not tamed nor ordinarily kept in captivity, is not property for the purpose of the Act unless it has been or is being reduced into possession.

Belonging to another

Section 5(1) of the Act describes possessory and proprietary rights rather than actual ownership. In *R v Turner (No 2)* (1971), the defendant took his car back from a garage without their knowledge while the car was taken there for repair. His intention was not to pay the bill. The court held that the fact that the defendant was the owner of the car was not a defence since the garage had possession and control of the car at the time.

Dishonesty

Section 2(1) provides three situations in which a defendant will not be regarded as dishonest:

(a) the defendant believes he has a legal right to the property (for example, an employer has not paid his employees' wages and the employees take goods);

(b) the defendant believes he has the consent of the person to which the property belongs;

(c) the defendant believes the person to whom the property belongs cannot be traced by taking reasonable steps (for example, a five pound note in an open street).

Intention to permanently deprive

It was understood that inclusion of the word 'permanently' would cause confusion. Section 6(1) of the 1968 Act explains that a person appropriating without meaning to permanently deprive the owner of the stolen item, is nevertheless to be regarded as having the intention of permanently depriving the other of it, if his intention is to treat the thing as his own, to dispose of, regardless of the other's rights or the period and circumstances of borrowing makes it equivalent to an outright taking or disposal. Therefore, taking a football club season ticket and returning it to the owner after a few games is theft. Taking goods from the owner with the intention to sell them back to him, though the owner will not be permanently deprived of the goods, is also theft. In *R v Lloyd* (1985), the defendant, a cinema projectionist, took films from the cinema to make pirate copies for sale. It was held that the defendant and his co-accused might have infringed others' copyright, but he had not committed theft because the films were returned without losing their 'goodness and virtue' and the cinema had not been permanently deprived of them.

Robbery

Section 8(1) of the 1968 Act provides that a person is guilty of robbery if he steals and immediately before, or at the time of doing so, and in order to do so, he uses force on any person or puts or seeks to put any person in fear of being there and then subject to force. In short, robbery means theft plus battery or assault. When there is no theft, there is no robbery. All five elements of theft have to be proved by the prosecution. In *R v Robinson* (1977), the defendant's conviction for robbery was quashed because he honestly believed that he was entitled to the property in question. Snatching a woman's handbag from behind can be said to have not put force nor fear on the victim, therefore, was only theft but not robbery. Maximum penalty for robbery is life imprisonment.

Burglary

Section 1(1) of the 1968 Act provides that a person is guilty of burglary if:

(a) he enters any building or part of a building as a trespasser and with intent to commit any such offences as is mentioned in sub-s (2); or

(b) having entered any building or part of a building as a trespasser he steals or attempts to steal ... or inflicts or attempts to inflict on any person therein any GBH.

The offences stated in sub-s (2) are theft, inflicting on any person any GBH, rape, doing unlawful damage to the building or anything therein (simply means 'in there').

When a person goes into a shop, he has an implied permission to enter from the shop owner; therefore, there is no trespass. If he steals in the shop, then he may be convicted for theft. But, if he jumps behind the counter or sneaks into the staff room (*the part of the building* to which the person has no permission to enter) and takes some money, he has committed the offence of burglary. Sub-section (a) describes the obvious situation when a person enters a building, or part of it, with an intention to commit certain crimes, and stipulates that he has committed burglary at the moment he made entry. It does not matter if he gets caught before he manages to steal anything. Sub-section (b) includes another situation where there is no criminally liable intention when a person enters the building. It is when he sees something and attempts to steal it that he has committed burglary. The maximum penalty for the offence is 14 years' imprisonment.

Aggravated burglary

Section 10 of the Theft Act 1968 provides that, if a person commits any burglary and at the time has with him any firearm or imitation firearm, any weapon of offence, or any explosive, he has committed the offence of aggravated burglary, which carries a maximum sentence of life imprisonment.

TWOC

Section 12 of the Theft Act 1968 contains an offence of taking a conveyance without the consent of the owner, commonly known as TWOC. This offence covers the situation where a joy rider argues that he has not stolen anything because he has left the car somewhere where it might be found and, therefore, he has no intention of permanently depriving the owner of the car. An offender of this crime includes a passenger who knows that he is being driven in a vehicle for which there is no consent. Conveyance does not only mean a car; it is defined in s 12(7)(a) as anything carrying a person or persons on land, water or air. Maximum penalty is three years' imprisonment. When the conveyance is a bicycle, the penalty is maximum £50 fine.

Some other offences under the Theft Acts

The following statutory offences may be outside of the GCSE syllabus, but students should be aware of their existence:

Theft Act 1968

- s 13:   dishonest use of electricity;
- s 15:   dishonestly obtaining property belonging to another by deception;
- s 15(4): a deception can be made deliberately or recklessly by words (for example, a false statement) or by conduct (for example, providing a wrong identity or bank cards) as to fact or to law. Maximum penalty is 10 years' imprisonment;
- s 16:   dishonestly obtaining a pecuniary advantage by deception. An example is to apply for a job with

fraudulent qualifications. Maximum penalty is five years' imprisonment;

- s 21: blackmail, maximum penalty is 14 years' imprisonment;
- s 22: handling stolen goods, maximum penalty is 14 years' imprisonment;
- s 25: going equipped for burglary, theft or deception, maximum penalty is three years' imprisonment;
- s 17: false accounting.

Theft Act 1978

- s 1: dishonestly obtaining services by deception;
- s 2: evasion of liability by deception;
- s 3: making off without payment for any goods supplied or services done.

Criminal damage

Section 1(1) of the Criminal Damage Act 1971 provides that, if a person destroys or damages, without lawful excuse, any property belonging to another, intentionally or recklessly, he has committed the offence of Criminal Damage, for which the maximum penalty is 10 years' imprisonment.

Section 1(2) is a similar offence but with further intention of endangering life.

Section 1(3) is the offence of arson in which the damage or destruction is caused by fire. These two more serious offences carry a maximum penalty of life imprisonment.

General defences

Specific crimes sometimes have their own specific defences, for example, provocation and diminished responsibility are specific defences for murder and are only available for murder. Therefore, it must be noted that there is no defence for a person being provoked into a fight, that is, assault and battery, though he may have a defence of self-defence. In many statutory offences, the legislation creating the offence may provide some conditions relying on which an accused may have a defence. Again, these are specific defences. General defences are those defences which, when appropriate, are applicable to all crimes. They include insanity, automatism, intoxication, mistake, duress and necessity.

Insanity and the M'Naghten Rules

If an accused suffers from mental disorder, he may be ordered to be detained in a hospital before a trial. During a trial, a jury may find him unfit to plead, and he may be further detained in a hospital.

In this section, we are discussing insanity as a general defence, which is available for a defendant when the trial proceeds. After the case of *M'Naghten* (1843), in which the accused was acquitted of murder on the grounds of insanity, it stimulated controversy. The House of Lords investigated the issue, then set out certain criteria regarding the defence of insanity which became known as the M'Naghten Rules. These Rules were later expressly reaffirmed by the case *R v Sullivan* (1984) and became the primary tests when insanity is pleaded. The Rules state that:

(a)   Every person is presumed to be sane and, therefore, responsible for his crime until the contrary is proved.

(b)   An accused must show that, at the time of committing the act, he is labouring under a defect of reason caused by a disease of the mind, and he does not know the nature and quality of the act, or, if he knows it, he does not know that he is doing wrong.

'Defect of reason' means the incapability of exercising a power of reasoning. 'Disease of the mind' is a disease, which affects the functioning of the mind, and refers to something internal, inherent or organic.

(c)   The responding act must fit the insane delusion. As quoted as an example in the *M'Naghten* investigation, if a defendant's delusion is that another man is attempting to take away his life and he kills that man, as he supposes, in self-defence, he would be exempt from punishment. If his delusion was that the deceased inflicted a serious injury to his character and fortune, and he killed him in revenge for such supposed injury, he would be liable for punishment.

If the defence is successfully pleaded, the verdict should be 'not guilty by reason of insanity'. It used to be the case that the person would be put into a psychiatric hospital indefinitely until a recommendation was given for his release, therefore, defendants were reluctant to plead such a defence. Since the Criminal Procedure (Insanity and Unfitness to Plead) Act 1991, the judge is given a range of options to either commit the person to a psychiatric hospital (still the only option for murder); to make a supervision order or guardianship order with or without treatment; or to order absolute discharge.

Automatism

Automatism is an involuntary act caused by non-inherent or external conditions such as an injury, a blow on the head or involuntary intoxication by drink and drugs. The involuntary act has to be committed totally out of the control of the accused's mind. It can be committed when the person is conscious (for example, a reflex action, spasm or convulsion) or unconscious (for example, concussion or sleepwalking). A classic example was given in the case of *Hill v Baxter* (1958) where the defendant was attacked by a swarm of bees when he was driving.

Lord Denning stated in the case of *Bratty v AG for Northern Ireland* (1963) that sleepwalking could be automatism. However, in *R v Burgess* (1991), it was held that a violent sleepwalker must be suffering from a disease of the mind, therefore, the accused was found not guilty by reason of insanity. It makes a big difference if a defendant can successfully prove automatism because the result of it will be an absolute acquittal.

Distinguishing insanity, diminished responsibility and automatism

Insanity is a defect of reason caused by a disease of the mind. Epilepsy is inherent and not caused by any external factors, therefore, is likely to be a disease of the mind. Sleepwalking can be automatism, but the court can also take the view that a violent sleepwalker must be suffering from a disease of mind. In *R v Quick* (1973), when the diabetic defendant injected too much insulin, causing a symptom of a hypo-glycaemia fit (due to extremely low sugar level in the blood), inflicted bodily harm to another, automatism was his defence because taking an excessive amount of insulin was an external factor. In *R v Hennessy* (1989), Hennessy was also a diabetic who had failed to take his dose of insulin and hence suffered from hyperglycaemia (excessive sugar content in the blood). It was held that his defence should be insanity because hyperglycaemia was an inherent defect.

'Diminished responsibility' is an abnormality of the mind arising from a condition of arrested or retarded development of the mind which can be anything inherent, induced by a disease or an injury. The scope is much wider than those of insanity and automatism. It must be noted that diminished responsibility is a specific defence for murder and is, therefore, only available for murder.

Intoxication

We have discussed earlier how involuntary intoxication can be a defence of automatism. We are concerned here with a possible defence of self-intoxication. In general, it is not a defence for crimes where the required *mens rea* is recklessness but may be a possible defence for specific intent crimes such as murder, s 18 wounding with intent and theft.

In *DPP v Majewski* (1976), the defendant was drunk when he assaulted a constable. He was convicted of assaulting a constable in the execution of his duty which offence only required recklessness. The *mens rea* for rape, as provided in s 1(1) of the Sexual Offences (Amendment) Act 1976, is either when the man intends to have non-consensual intercourse or he is reckless as to whether or not the woman is consenting. Recklessness is sufficient to convict and, therefore, the Court of Appeal held in *R v Fotheringham* (1989) that intoxication (being drunk in this case) is no defence for rape. In *R v Lipman* (1970), the defendant killed a girl when under the influence of LSD and was only guilty of manslaughter since murder requires specific intent. It appears that the result would be the same if the defendant was under the influence of alcohol. It would not be the same if a person took a drink to pluck up the courage to kill. This was the ratio given in the case of *AG for Northern Ireland v Gallagher* (1961).

In *R v Hardie* (1984), the defendant took five tablets of Valium then burnt down a flat. It was found that, although the intoxication was self induced, the defendant had the excuse of not knowing the effect of taking the Valium. The Court of Appeal quashed his conviction for criminal damage though the offence only requires recklessness. The court held that the defendant lacked *mens rea*. It appears that, where soporific or sedative drugs are involved, the courts are prepared to widen the scope of intoxication as a defence.

As a conclusion, the courts will consider the following issues when faced with a defence of intoxication:

(a) Was it an involuntary or self-induced intoxication?

(b) If it was the latter, did and should the defendant have known the effects of the substance taken? Was it a genuine mistake? If so, the defendant may have a defence of lack of *mens rea* or automatism.

(c)   If it was self-induced, and the defendant should have known the effects, it may be a defence for specific intent crimes, but not for offence which only require recklessness to convict.

Mistake

Ignorance of the law is no defence; therefore, a mistake of law is no defence either. It is a mistake of fact which can help a defendant because it shows that he lacks the *mens rea* required.

For crimes of strict liability and those which can be committed negligently, the mistake has to be reasonable and honest. This principle is created in the case of *R v Tolson* (1889), where Mrs Tolson was found not guilty of bigamy because she honestly and reasonably believed that her husband was dead. In *DPP v Morgan* (1975), it was further established that, for other crimes, a mistake has to be honest, but does not have to be reasonable.

Duress and necessity

In *AG v Whelan* (1934), Murnaghan J defined duress as 'threats of immediate death or serious personal violence so great as to overbear the ordinary powers of human resistance'. The courts try to encourage people to resist pressure to commit crimes and, therefore, have limited the scope for duress. Anything less than the above stated can rarely suffice especially for more serious crimes. It has been clearly recognised that duress is no defence for murder (*R v Howe* (1987)), attempted murder (*R v Gotts* (1991)) and some form of treason (*R v Oldcastle* (1419)).

Duress and necessity are similar in the way that they put a person in a situation where he has to make a choice between two evils. The traditional distinction between these two defences is that necessity is a circumstance and duress is a threat made by another person. Until a series of cases in the 1980s, there was little doubt that necessity could only be used as mitigation (that is, plea for lower sentence after the accused has pleaded or been found guilty). This is illustrated in the classic case of *R v Dudley and Stephens* (1884). In this case, three men and a cabin boy were shipwrecked and, after about 20 days in an open boat, the defendants killed the boy and ate his flesh to survive. The accused were convicted for murder, however, the sentence was ultimately commuted to six months imprisonment. There were a series of cases (*R v Willer* (1986), *R v Conway* (1989) and *R v Martin* (1989)) in which the courts came to recognise a situation of 'duress of circumstances'. These cases involved motoring offences where Willer drove on the pavement in order to escape from a gang of youths whom he thought to be violent. Conway drove off at speed intending to escape from two potential assassins of his passenger (in fact, they were police officers). Martin drove while disqualified because his wife, who was known to have suicidal tendencies, threatened to kill herself if he did not drive their son to work. However, it was further held in these cases that a defendant could only escape liability if he acted with reasonable firmness. In *R v Pommell* (1995), the courts further demonstrated their willingness to allow 'duress of circumstances' to cases other than motoring offences.

As a result of these cases:

- it would be very difficult to distinguish between duress and necessity as a defence and it may be more correct to say that there is no need to distinguish between the two defences now;

- the law keeps developing in these areas. However, it should remain settled that duress and necessity are no defence for murder, attempted murder and some forms of treason.

Self-defence

The common law permits a person to use reasonable force to defend himself or someone else against attack, or to protect his or another's property. This has now largely been superseded by s 3(1) of the Criminal Law Act 1967, which allows the use of reasonable force in order to prevent crime or to arrest offenders or suspects or persons unlawfully at large. What is reasonable force depends upon the circumstances.

4 Contract Law

You should be familiar with the following areas:

- the essentials of contract and the effects of the absence of them
- rules relating to offer, acceptance and invitation to treat
- use of postal and other means of communication on offer and acceptance
- rules of consideration
- distinction of legal intention to contract on domestic and social agreements
- capacity of minors to make contracts and the effect of the Minors' Contracts Act 1987
- discharge of contract by frustration and the effects of the Law Reform (Frustrated Contracts) Act 1943
- breach of contract and the remedies
- consumer contract and related provisions under various statutes
- duties of employer and employee, sex and racial discrimination in employment

Introduction

A contract is an agreement between two or more parties, who promise to give and receive something from each other and who intend that the agreement be legally binding. Except for some special contracts, for example, sale of a house, there is no general legal requirement that a contract has to be in writing. Verbal contracts are as enforceable as written contracts. The problem with verbal contracts is not on validity but on evidence. When nothing is recorded in black and white it is difficult to prove who has said what.

Contract law is categorised in the law of obligation. A contract creates a legal obligation between the contracting parties. When one party has not fulfilled, or is not going to fulfil the obligation, he can be sued for breach of contract. The court will help the innocent party by either ordering damages suffered to be compensated, compelling the party in breach to perform the contract (specific performance order) or prohibiting the wrongdoer to act in a way which would cause further breaches (injunction order). It is therefore important to know how and when a binding agreement has been created. The following are six main essentials for a contract to be formed, they are:

- offer and acceptance;
- consideration;
- intention to create legal relationship;
- capacity;
- legality;
- *consensus ad idem* (meeting of minds).

For a contract to exist, the first three essentials have to be present. Without any of them, no contract has been formed in the first place. It is quite different when any of the latter three essentials is absent. If a party who lacks legal capacity, for example, a minor, makes a contract, the law recognises the contract, but may also intervene by giving the minor the option to avoid the contract. Therefore, the contract is not void, but is said to be voidable. If a contract is made with an illegal objective, the court will not enforce the contract, in other words, there is a contract, but it is unenforceable. When a person enters into a contract caused by fraud, misrepresentation, a serious mistake, duress or undue influence, there is, in effect, no meeting of minds. In some cases, the contracts are void and in others they may be voidable.

Offer

Sir Guenter Treitel in his book, *The Law of Contract*, defines an offer as an expression of willingness to contract on certain terms made with the intention that it shall become binding as soon as it is accepted by the person to whom it is addressed.

There are further rules, mostly created by common law, relating to 'offer'. These are:

Offer must be communicated to the offeree

An offer is an expression of willingness to contract and it must be expressed or communicated to a person, otherwise the person cannot accept something he is unaware of. For example, a reward has been offered for returning a lost item. If a person returns the item and, at the time, he does not know of the offer, then the offeror is not liable to reward him because he has not accepted anything and, therefore, there was no contract binding the parties.

Offer may be made to the whole world

In *Carlill v Carbolic Smoke Ball Company* (1893), Carbolic Smoke Ball issued an advertisement stating that they would pay £100 to anyone who contracted influenza after using their smoke balls. Mrs Carlill saw the advertisement, bought and used the smoke ball but still caught influenza. She claimed the award but was refused. Amongst other things, Carbolic argued that offers had to be communicated to specific individuals. The court held that an offer could be made to the whole world, that is, everybody, as well as a particular individual or group of persons.

Offers may be made in writing, orally or by conduct

An example of making an offer by conduct is the raising of one's hand at an auction. The acceptance occurs when the hammer hits the table. Another example is when goods are placed on a checkout at a supermarket. There is no need for the person to say to the shop assistant 'I am offering to buy these items'. However, some contracts are required by law to be made in writing or even on a prescribed form. The Law of Property (Miscellaneous Provisions) Act (1989) states that contract for the sale of land or other disposition of an interest in land must be in writing. This includes the selling of a piece of land, a house, a lease and many other interests relating to land. The Consumer Credit Act (1974) stipulates that consumer credit agreements, such as hire purchase, personal loan, credit cards, overdraft agreements, etc, must also be made in writing. Further, there are detailed regulations governing the contents of these agreements. If a regulated agreement is improperly concluded, the creditor cannot enforce it unless a court order is obtained.

Invitation to treat is not an offer

It may be said that an invitation to treat is only an expression of willingness to enter into negotiation and the invitor has no intention of being bound until the final agreement is reached. An invitation to treat comes in many forms, outlined below.

Supplying information is distinguishable from an offer

In *Harvey v Facey* (1893), Harvey enquired whether Facey would consider selling his Bumper Hall pen and what the lowest price would be. Facey replied stating that the lowest price would be £900. Harvey 'accepted' at that price but Facey refused to sell. The court held that Facey was supplying information when indicating the lowest price. It was not an offer, but only an invitation to treat and, therefore, there was no binding contract. In other words, an invitation to treat is not capable of being accepted. In *Gibson v Manchester City Council* (1979), the council wrote to Gibson stating that the council might be prepared to sell the house to him at the price of £2,725 less 20%. Gibson made an application on that basis, but, later, the council withdrew from the sale. Gibson claimed that a contract had come into existence, but the court held that the council's earlier letter was only an invitation to treat and Gibson's later application was the offer which had not been accepted. In the commercial world, many negotiations are conducted on 'I am prepared' or 'subject to contract' basis and one should not presume that an agreement has been reached until a confirmation is obtained.

Self-service shops

Pharmaceutical Society of Great Britain v Boots Cash Chemists (Southern) Ltd (1952) dealt with the question 'Is displaying goods in a self-service shop an offer or only an invitation to treat?' In the case, Boots operated a self-service system in their shops and they were accused of selling listed drugs without the supervision of a registered pharmacist. The court held that an offer did not take place until a customer took the drugs to the cash desk where a pharmacist operated. It is only an invitation to treat when an item is displayed on the shelf with its price tag. Boots was found not guilty of the accusation. The same principle applies when we buy goods in shops and supermarkets these days. If the wrong price tag is attached to an item and a customer takes it to the till, the shop assistant is entitled to refuse to sell it at the incorrect price. The parties are not legally bound until the shop assistant has accepted the offer.

Display in shop window

In *Fisher v Bell* (1961), a flick knife, which was illegal, was displayed in the defendant's shop window and he was accused of offering for sale an offensive weapon contrary to the Restriction of Offensive Weapons Act 1959. The court held that displaying goods in a shop window was only an invitation to treat and, therefore, the defendant had not 'offered' the weapon for sale and, hence, he was not guilty.

Advertisement

In *Partridge v Crittenden* (1968), the appellant was accused of offering for sale a live wild bird contrary to the Protection of Birds Act 1954. He placed an advertisement in a periodical to sell his 'Bramblefinch cocks and hens'. The appeal was allowed since the court held that advertisements in general are invitations to treat, not offers. The principle remains nowadays so that when a shop runs out of stock one cannot make a claim against the shop for advertising their goods with a price in a newspaper. The case is distinguishable from *Carlill v Carbolic Smoke Ball* where the wording was specific and was intended to be understood by the public as an offer which was to be acted upon. The principle in *Carlill* will probably apply if an advertisement says the first two customers to buy an ABC 33 inch wide screen TV in the shop today will only pay £10!

Commercial tender

In general, an invitation to tender is an invitation to treat and a tender submitted is the offer. However, it was held in *Blackpool and Fylde Aero Club v Blackpool BC* (1990) that, if the invitation is addressed to specified parties, the invitor has a duty to consider each tender seriously and fairly.

Acceptance

Once an offer is accepted and other essentials are present, a contract is formed. The parties can no longer change their minds.

Acceptance must be unqualified

When an offeree seeks to change the terms of an offer, he has passed the initiative back to the offeror. In *Hyde v Wrench* (1840), where Wrench offered to sell his farm at £1,000. Hyde counter offered to buy the farm at £950, but Wrench refused that. Hyde later accepted the original offer of £1,000 but Wrench changed his mind. Hyde sued and the court held that his earlier counter offer destroyed the original offer, so there was nothing there for him to accept. A counter offer must, however, be distinguished from an enquiry for further information. In the case of *Stevenson v McLean* (1880), the offeree enquired whether credit would be given for payment. After refusal of credit, he accepted the original offer and the court upheld the contract because, when the offeree inquired for credit, he was requesting further information which is not a counter offer. The position was different in *Neale v Merrett* (1930) where Merrett offered to sell at £280. Neale replied, purporting to accept the offer. He also enclosed £80 and further promised to pay £50 per month. The court held that the acceptance was a qualified one, departing from the original offer, and, therefore, there was no contract. It can be appreciated that one has to be quite careful in conducting oneself in business when closing a deal.

Acceptance must be communicated to the offeror

Acceptance can be written, oral or made by conduct, but it must be communicated to the offeror. There are exceptions, however, an example being the *Carlill* case again. One of the arguments of the case was that Mrs Carlill never communicated her acceptance to the offeror before claiming her £100 and, therefore, there was no contract in the first place. The court held that acceptance may be implied from the conduct of the acceptor and the need for the acceptance communication may be waived. In *Felthouse v Bindley* (1862), Felthouse made an offer to his nephew stating 'If I hear no more from you, I consider the horse to be mine'. The court held that silence cannot be imposed on an offeree as an acceptance, but may be treated as a waiver of acceptance communication. The effect is that the offeree may enforce the contract against the offeror but not vice versa.

Acceptance must be in the mode as specified in the offer

In *Eliason v Henshaw* (1819), Eliason made an offer to buy flour, which also stipulated that acceptance must be given to the wagoner who delivered the offer. The acceptance was sent by post and was received after the wagoner's return. The court held that there was no contract because the specific mode of acceptance was not followed. Sometimes, the court may relax this rule slightly, as in *Manchester Diocean Council for Education v Commercial and General Investments Ltd* (1969), where the acceptance for the sale of land was sent to the owner's surveyors instead of the owner as prescribed. This was held to be valid since it was equally expeditious and had not put the offeror in a less advantageous position. In *Quenerduaine v Cole* (1883), there was no method of acceptance stated in the offer, which was made by telegram. Acceptance by post was held to be not sufficient. The *ratio* of the case is that the method of acceptance is inferred by the manner in which an offer is made and, therefore, a method of acceptance which may prejudice the interest of the offeror can be invalid.

The postal rule

If postal communication is used, an offer is effective when it is received. An acceptance is effective as soon as the letter is posted, not when it is received. This rule was laid down by cases during the 19th century, such as *Adams v Lindsell* (1818). This postal rule even extends to letters which have never been received. In *Household Fire Insurance Co v Grant* (1879), Grant applied to purchase shares of the company. The company accepted the offer, but the letter never reached Grant. The company later went into liquidation and the liquidator demanded Grant to pay up for the shares. The Court of Appeal upheld the postal rule, that is, acceptance took place as soon as the letter was posted. The liquidator won the case. The postal rule on acceptance was not free from criticism but it did, however, became widely accepted with the justification that the post office is considered to be an agent of offerors to receive acceptance. Offerors should be aware of the risks inherent in the use of the post and they can always expressly exclude the rule. By stating that an acceptance shall be by notice in writing, an offeror has prescribed a method of communication, that is, the offeror must have actual communication of the acceptance and, hence, has excluded the postal rule (*Holwell Securities Ltd v Hughes* (1974)).

Instantaneous modes of communication

In *Entores Ltd v Miles Far East Corporation* (1955), it was held that a contract is completed in the receiving country and is concluded when the telex is received. The former ratio is important for international trade when deciding which country's law should take effect for a particular contract when the contract is silent on this issue. In *Brinkibon v Stahag Stahl GmbH* (1983), it was further held that a contract is completed when it may be read the next working morning if a telex acceptance is received out of office hours. It is generally accepted that the above principle should be applied to other instantaneous forms of communication such as fax, telephone answering machine and likely email.

Termination of an offer

An acceptance after an offer is terminated will not be effective. An offer will come to an end when the offeree rejects the offer or makes a counter offer. An offer is also terminated when it is revoked or withdrawn by the offeror. The length of time in which an offer is valid may be stated in the offer itself. If no such time is stipulated, and the offer has not been revoked, it could still be automatically revoked after a reasonable period of time. In *Ramsgate Victoria Hotel v Monte Fiore* (1866), it was too late to accept an offer to purchase shares after six months had lapsed.

An offer may be withdrawn at any time before an acceptance. Such revocation must be communicated to the offeree. If revocation is made by post, it is effective when received *not* when posted (*Byrne v Van Tienhoven* (1880)). It should be noted that an offeror could not withdraw an offer if consideration was given to keep the offer open for a period of time. Later sections will explain the meaning of consideration. An offer will also be terminated by the death of either party unless the acceptor does not know of the offeror's death and the personal representative can perform the contract.

Cross-offer

A cross-offer occurs when both parties send identical offers to each other. A makes an offer to buy B's car for £3,000 and, at the same time, B sends his offer to A to sell his car for £3,000. A contract must possess an offer and an acceptance and in the example there is no contract because there has not been an acceptance. This is the situation when there is a meeting of minds but no binding contract yet.

Consideration

What is consideration?

It is said that an Englishman is liable, not because he has made a promise, but because he has made a bargain. A binding contract is one in which a party takes something in return for giving something else – this is the bargain. The 'giving' and 'taking' are the consideration in a contract. Consideration is the price of a bargain, which does not have to be money, but must have some value in the eyes of the law. It may be some detriment to the promisee or some benefit to the promisor (*Thomas v Thomas* (1842)). It can be 'some right, interest, profit or benefit accruing to one party, or some forbearance, detriment, loss or responsibility given, suffered or undertaken by the other' (*Currie v Misa* (1875)). For example, A agrees to work in B's shop for B forgetting A's debt to him. Working for B is a detriment to A and a benefit for B. Forgetting A's debt is a legal right being forfeited. This agreement is supported by consideration from both sides and is, therefore, a binding contract. A contract is binding, but gifts are not. It is important to distinguish between the two. If one side has not provided consideration, there is no contract. If A promises to give £100 to B for nothing in return and later A changes his mind, A may be morally wrong, but B cannot sue A for he has not provided consideration. There are however some exceptions. A gift, if made by deed, is binding.

Nature of consideration

Consideration must be sufficient but need not be adequate
If A promised to give £100 to B for his old GCSE law book, this is not simply a gift. The old book does not appear to be adequate in return for £100 but, in the eyes of the law, it has some value and is, therefore, sufficient. The agreement has created a right for A to possess the book and it is binding. In the case of *Chappell and Co Ltd v Nestlé Co Ltd* (1960), the House of Lords held that wrappers from three bars of chocolate were sufficient consideration.

Consideration must be more than an existing duty
If a solicitor is promised extra money to handle a case to the best of his ability, this is not enforceable because lawyers are supposed to do their best anyway. If the extra money is for working extra hours, then this

promise is enforceable because the consideration here is more than an existing duty.

In *Stilk v Myrick* (1809), two sailors deserted their ship and the captain promised the rest of the crew extra wages. When the ship sailed home, the promise was not honoured. The court held that the crew was bound by their contract to meet any 'normal' emergencies of the voyage and their consideration to sail the ship home had not exceeded their existing contractual duty and, therefore, the promise was not an enforceable agreement. This case must be distinguished from *Hartley v Ponsonby* (1857) where half of the crew abandoned the ship. The court held that the consideration of the rest of the crew had exceeded their existing duty and, therefore, they were entitled to the extra money promised. The same principle applies in debt cases where a subsequent agreement to pay a smaller sum does not legally discharge the debtor to repay the debt in full. A owes B £1,000 and the repayment is due. A negotiates with B and they agree on a repayment of £800, which A pays. B then later goes back and demands the extra £200. He is legally entitled to do so because A has not provided good consideration for the subsequent agreement, he was obliged to pay the £800 anyway. This is a principle laid down by the *Pinnel's Case* (1602), which was confirmed by the House of Lords in *Foakes v Beer* (1884).

However, under certain exceptional circumstances, an existing obligation can be good consideration. The late Lord Denning, in the case of *Central London Property Trust Ltd v High Trees House Ltd* (1947), set out the circumstances that are required before this doctrine of promissory estoppel operates. The law in this area has been quite clear until the recent case of *Williams v Roffey Brothers and Nicholls* (1990). Sub-contractor Williams was contracted to carry out carpentry work for 27 flats for the main contractor, Roffey Brothers, at a fixed price. When half of the flats were completed, Williams got into financial difficulty and realised that the agreed price was too low. They slowed down the work. Roffey Brothers could foresee late completion which would also result in heavy penalties against them, so they promised additional money to Williams for them to complete the work in time (that is, their existing duty). Ultimately, Roffey Brothers failed to pay as promised. The Court of Appeal held that Roffey Brothers had obtained new practical benefits and avoided a disadvantage, which amounted to good considerations. This decision has, however, departed from the rule that existing duty cannot be sufficient consideration and has, therefore, thrown this area of law back into confusion. Regrettably, the case was settled between the parties after the appeal in the Court of Appeal and the House of Lords did not have an opportunity to clarify the law.

Past consideration is not good consideration

In *Re McArdle* (1951), the plaintiff had executed some house improvements then the owner promised to pay the costs. He did not do so and the plaintiff took legal action. The court held that the consideration of doing the improvement work had been executed before the defendant promised to pay and was, therefore, past consideration and the agreement had not been supported by good consideration. It would be different if the defendant requested the service in the first place and there was inferred intention at the time that the service should be remunerated. The latter principle is the *ratio* in *Lampleigh v Braithwait* (1615) and a more recent Hong Kong case of *Pao On v Lau Yiu Long* (1979).

Privity of contract

This doctrine states that a person who is not a party to a contract is not entitled to sue because he has not provided consideration. For example, A agrees with B that, if B finishes the work, A will give £100 to C. If A later does not pay C, C cannot sue A. The correct party to sue is B.

However, under the Contracts (Rights of Third Parties) Act 1999, C is given a right to sue A for breach of contract. The purpose of the Act is to give a third party a right to enforce a contract provided the contract conferred a benefit on them.

Intention to create legal relationship

For an agreement to be legally binding, the parties must intend it to be so.

The law presumes that social or domestic promises and agreements do not possess such an intention, however, this presumption will be rebutted if the intention to create a legal relationship is expressed. In *Simpkins v Pays* (1955), Simpkins jointly with Pays and her granddaughter entered into a weekly coupon competition. One week, they won prize money of £750. Simpkins was not paid and had to sue for his share of £250. The court held that there was evidence which showed that the parties were engaged in a joint enterprise and the arrangement was not a mere domestic one. In *Balfour v Balfour* (1919), the court refused to enforce an agreement that the wife was to be paid £50 per month while the husband worked abroad. However, when a couple are separating or separated, as in *Merritt v Merritt* (1970), the courts are prepared to enforce a clear agreement between the parties.

For commercial agreements, it is presumed that there is an intention to be legally bound unless expressed otherwise. Many football pools coupons contain notes stating 'binding in honour only' or 'it shall not give rise to any legal relationship' no action can be taken against an unpaid win (*Jones v Vernons Pools Ltd* (1938) and *Appleson v Littlewood Ltd* (1939)). In *Rose and Frank v Crompton* (1925), there was a clause in the business agreement stating: '... this arrangement is not ... a formal or legal agreement and shall not be subject to legal jurisdiction in the law courts.' The court held that the parties had expressed their intention not to be legally bound and, therefore, the agreement was not an enforceable contract.

Capacity

As a general rule, any person can enter into a binding contract. However, the law recognises that a person of young age or mental deficiency may not be able to fully appreciate the effects of a contract and may easily be taken advantage of by more experienced persons, rules are therefore formed for the protection of these classes of persons. Another aspect in this area of law is concerned with the capacity of an organisation to make contracts. Corporations and other organisations can exist in various forms such as limited company, chartered corporation, statutory corporation, charity organisation, association and club. Their constitutions sometimes limit the scope of contract into which they can enter. It should be understood that, if an organisation has no authority to make certain contracts, such contracts made may be void. Further aspects of these rules are outside the scope of this book and we shall now concentrate on the area which relates to the legal effects on contracts made by minors.

Minors

The Family Law Reform Act 1969 provides that, from 1 January 1970, minors are those persons who are under 18 years old (previously 21). The Minors' Contracts Act 1987 repealed the Infants Relief Act 1874, which rendered 'absolutely void' all contracts with minors for the payment of money lent, or for goods supplied or to be supplied other than contracts for 'necessaries'. The effect after the Minors' Contracts Act 1987 is that all contracts with a minor are only voidable except for (a) contracts for necessaries; and (b) beneficial contracts of service, which are binding between the minor and the other party (or parties). Contracts for necessaries are contracts for: '... goods suitable to the condition in life of the minor and to his requirements at the time of sale and delivery' as defined in s 3 of the Sale of Goods Act 1979. Examples of necessaries include such obvious things like food, clothing and medical attention. Other services such as legal advice or car hire may also be included, depending on the circumstances.

In *Nash v Inman* (1908), a Cambridge undergraduate, a minor, ordered 11 fancy waistcoats but failed to pay. The tailor sued but it was shown that the defendant was supplied with adequate clothes suitable for his condition in life when the waistcoats were delivered. The court held that the order was not a contract for necessaries and the action failed. In *Chapple v Cooper* (1844), a minor's widow contracted through an undertaker for a funeral of her deceased husband. It was held that the funeral arrangements were necessary.

Beneficial contracts of service, under the common law, are those contracts including training, education, apprenticeship and other similar contracts, which are binding against the minor if, taken as a whole, they are for the benefit of the minor. In *De Francesco v Barnum* (1890), a minor entered into an apprenticeship as a dancer. The training contract provided that she would not marry, would receive no pay and would not dance professionally without the tutor's consent. When there was a dispute, and the matter was put in front of the court, the court examined the contract and held that it was unreasonably harsh and, as a whole, was not for the minor's benefit. The dancer was entitled to avoid the contract.

All other contracts, outside the two groups mentioned above, are voidable at the minor's option. If repudiated, the minor must pay for the benefit received, not necessarily at the agreed price, but at a reasonable price that the court thinks fit. Section 3 of the 1987 Act allows the other party, when just and reasonable, to recover from the minor any property acquired under the contract or any other property representing it. This means that, if an item has been supplied to a minor and he has avoided the contract, the other party is entitled to the return of the item. If the minor has sold the item for £100, or exchanged it for some other goods and is still in possession of the money or goods, the other party can obtain a court order for the transfer of the money or goods to him.

Section 2 of the same Act also makes a guarantee of a minor's contractual obligation enforceable against the guarantor, even though the main contract itself has been avoided. Finally, it should be noted that long term contracts relating to land, shares in companies and partnerships in business, if not repudiated, would be binding when the minor reaches maturity (that is, 18 years of age).

Legality

The rule is that no court action will arise from an illegal act and, therefore, a contract in relation to an illegal act, or for an illegal purpose, is void and no person can recover anything from it. Therefore, an agreement concerned with the commission of an act that is wrong at law, including, but not limited to, a contract for committing a crime is unenforceable. Likewise, agreements which are contrary to public policy, such as contracts to corrupt public life (*Parkinson v College of Ambulance* (1925)) and contracts promoting immorality (*Pearce v Brook* (1866)).

Consensus *ad idem* (meeting of minds)

When a contract would not have been agreed but for any fraud, misrepresentation, serious mistake, duress or undue influence, there is no meeting of minds in the first place. The law treats some of these contracts as void and some others voidable, allowing the innocent parties to avoid the contract if desired.

Discharge of contract

This simply means that a validly formed contract has come to an end. It may occur when:

(a) performed;
(b) further agreed by the parties;
(c) a party has breached a condition of the contract;
(d) the contract is frustrated (or subsequently impossible to perform).

Performance

This is when the contract comes to its end as agreed. It may be that the parties have carried out their promises or that the contract has come to the end of its term. There is, however, one particular situation which should be recognised, that is, substantial performance. This represents the situation where a party has carried out the contract only subject to some minor defects. Under the circumstances, the other party cannot claim for breach of contract. For example, a contractor was engaged to decorate the whole of a mansion house. The work was 'substantially completed' but two corners remained unpainted and a couple of shelves had not been fixed. The owners decided to put these right themselves. At the end, they could not claim that the decorator had breached the contract, but are entitled to have a reasonable sum deducted from the price.

Agreement

This is the situation when the parties agree to discharge the contract even though it has not been performed. Where neither side has performed their obligations under the contract, the parties may discharge the contract by waivers, meaning that they shall waive their rights and release each other from their obligations. If one side releases the other from the original obligation for a fresh consideration, the contract is said to have discharged by 'accord and satisfaction'. If there is no fresh consideration, the discharge must be made by deed for it to be legally effective.

Breach

In order to understand this topic, it must be understood that terms in a contract can be categorised into conditions and warranties. Conditions are the important terms of a contract. They go to the root of an agreement. A breach of a condition entitles the injured party to immediately repudiate (that is, terminate) the contract and sue for damages. For a breach of a warranty, the innocent party has no right to repudiate the contract (that is, it still has to run its term) but only a right to claim damages (for example, reduction of the price). It is important to distinguish conditions from warranties because, if the 'innocent party' has wrongfully repudiated a contract, the party may be subject to a claim or counter claim. A breach is not only restricted to failing to perform, merely showing an intention not to perform the legal obligation will suffice. In the event that a breach of condition occurs, the innocent party has two choices: he may either repudiate the contract, as mentioned above, or treat the contract as still subsisting and sue for damages later. If he chooses to do the latter, he must fulfil his side of the obligation until the end, otherwise he will also be in breach. For details regarding the remedies for breach of contract, see later sections.

Frustration (or subsequent impossibility)

The common law rules on contractual obligations are strict. It used to be the case that, when a contractual duty became impossible to carry out, the party would be regarded as having breached the contract. However, since the case of *Taylor v Caldwell* (1863), the courts have recognised, without any fault of either party, some events as being sufficient to render performance impossible. The contract is then automatically discharged and the parties can be excused from further performance. A contract can be frustrated by:

- *Destruction of a thing necessary for performance*

  In *Taylor v Caldwell* (1863), a music hall was hired but it was destroyed by fire without the fault of any parties.

- *Personal incapacity in contract for personal services*

  In *Robinson v Davison* (1871), a piano player was ill on the day of the performance.

- *Failure of some event which is the basis of the contract*

  In *Krell v Henry* (1903), a contract of hire for a room to watch the procession of Edward VII's coronation was frustrated since the King was ill and the event was cancelled. This, however, should be contrasted with *Herne Bay Steamboat Company v Hutton* (1903). Hutton hired a boat to view the fleet which was assembled to be reviewed by the King after the coronation. The court held that, even though the coronation was cancelled, the fleet was still assembled and, therefore, the contract was possible and, hence, not frustrated. Hutton had to pay.

- *Subsequent legislation rendering the performance impossible or illegal*

  In *Re Shipton Anderson and Co* (1915), the parties were contracted for delivery of wheat and it was frustrated by a subsequent Act of Parliament requisitioning all wheat for the government.

Throughout the years, the courts have been careful to keep the doctrine of frustration within a narrow limit. It has been established that a contract will not be frustrated:

(a)   on the grounds of inconvenience or increase in expenses;

(b)   when the impossibility is self-induced (that is, there is fault of a party);

(c)   when the event was foreseeable.

Effect of frustration
Under the old common law rule, it was the case that, when a contract was frustrated, it was automatically discharged at once and the parties are not obliged to carry out any further action or transaction. This could create harsh and unfair situations. When a party paid a deposit, and the contract was frustrated without the other side having done anything, the deposit could not be recovered. Continuing services or supplies had been made, but payment was not due until the end of term. In the meantime, if the contract could not be carried out, the receiver did not need to pay for the benefit already received. The Law Reform (Frustrated Contracts) Act 1943 changed this position and provides that:

(1)   money or property paid or passed over may be recoverable;

(2)   money payable before frustration ceases to be payable;

(3)   expenses incurred may be claimed out of the money paid beforehand or the amount payable;

(4)   the court may award a reasonable sum to be paid by one party who has gained a benefit from the work done by the other party.

It should be noted that the flexibility of the Act leaves plenty of room for the court to make appropriate orders. The Act does not apply to:

(a)   contracts which contain special provisions in the event of frustration which are sometimes called 'force majeure clauses';

(b)   contracts where the parties intend them to remain binding irrespective of frustrating events (that is, absolute agreements);

(c)   charter parties;

(d)   carriage of goods by sea; and

(e)   insurance contracts.

Remedies for breach of contract

Repudiation and damages

As discussed in an earlier section, when a party has breached a condition of a contract, the innocent party is entitled to, either repudiate the contract immediately and sue for damages, or consider the contract still subsisting and make appropriate claims later. In most cases, there can be proceedings to claim for damages.

Damages are said to be a common law remedy. The objective is to place the injured party into the position as if the contract had been completed so far as it is financially possible to do so. The damages awardable should not be too remote. This includes the loss of a bargain. For example, A paid £500 for goods and, on non-delivery (the breach), A has to pay £700 to replace what he intended to purchase. The damage is not only for the price of the contract of £500 but for £700. A has lost the bargain and the defendant has to compensate as if the goods were delivered. If this was a commercial deal (and understandably the claimant was going to sell the goods for a profit) and A can prove that, normally, he could resell them for £900, then the damage will be £900. The extent to which damages are awarded, and are regarded as too remote, was first enunciated in *Hadley v Baxendale* (1854). Baxendale contracted to deliver a crankshaft for Hadley's mill but the delivery was late. Hadley sued for loss of profit during the idle time of the mill. The court recognised that there was a breach, but also took the view that the damage claimed was too remote. It further set out the principle that damages for breach of contract should be awarded where: (a) they arise naturally from the breach itself; or (b) they were reasonably supposed to have been in contemplation of both parties at the time they made the contract.

Applying these principles in our previous example, supposing that A is a keen investor, he could not, however, claim that, if he had the £900 upon reselling the goods, he was going to invest in the stock market and since then he could have increased his investment to £1,500. This further damage does not arise naturally from the contract and is, therefore, too remote. Let's suppose A is an individual not normally engaged in buying and selling the goods. It might be his intention to resell the goods when he made the contract, but if the seller was not told of this intention, A cannot claim for the lost profit (damage of £900 resale price) because it had not been in the contemplation of the parties at the time of the contract. This is reasonable because, if B knows of the risk, he might want a higher price. A may only be entitled to the replacement price of £700.

The *Hadley v Baxendale* principle was confirmed by later cases. In *Victoria Laundry v Newman Industries Ltd* (1948), the laundry was able to recover damages for normal loss of profit following a delay in the delivery of a boiler, but not for special loss arising from some especially lucrative dyeing contract that they were offered during the time. Such damages were said to be not 'reasonably foreseeable' either from imputed or actual knowledge.

There is a legal duty for a claimant to take reasonable steps to mitigate his loss. Going back to our example, if it can be shown that A could have easily purchased a replacement for £600, the damage would only be £600, not £700 which he actually paid without taking reasonable steps to shop around.

Specific performance
Specific performance is an order by which the court compels a party to carry out the contract. This is an equitable remedy and is available when the common law remedies, normally damages, are inadequate. This is not uncommon in contracts for sale of land or interest in land.

Injunction
Injunction is also an equitable remedy which is designed to stop a party from causing a breach. This is sometimes available for contracts for personal services. In *Warner Brothers v Nelson* (1937), the film star Bette Davies was injuncted from making another movie for another production company while she was contracted with Warner Brothers at the time.

Rescission
Rescission is an equitable remedy which is commonly used in misrepresentation cases. The objective of rescission, which is slightly different from that for damages, is to place the parties in their pre-contractual position, for example, by returning the goods delivered or the money received.

Contracts and the consumer

The background
The English law doctrine of *'caveat emptor'* (let the buyer beware) placed the burden on a consumer to examine and be satisfied with the quality of the goods before a purchase. This has created unsatisfactory

results, especially in this modern age of technology. Consumers cannot be expected to have fully examined more and more sophisticated products before they purchase them. The Sale of Goods Act 1979 was consolidated to confer certain rights to consumers and to place them on a more equal standing when dealing with more professional and experienced business organisations.

What is covered by the Sale of Goods Act?

Section 2(1) defines that a sale of goods contract is a contract whereby a seller transfers, or agrees to transfer, the ownership of goods to a buyer for a money consideration called 'price'. This also includes those sales where the consideration is partly in money.

The scope for what goods are is very wide, however, and it is understood that they do not include land, exchange of goods, legal rights such as debts, copyrights, patents or trademarks. There are conditions and warranties implied by the Act on various consumer contracts. 'Implied' means that, even though a term has not been expressly agreed between the parties, it is automatically injected into the contract as long as it is covered by the Act. We have come across the terms 'conditions' and 'warranties' in an earlier section. Conditions are those important terms which go to the root of the contract in breach of which will entitle the innocent party to repudiate the contract and claim for damages. Warranties are those less important terms in breach of which will not entitle the innocent party to repudiate the contract but will allow him to claim for some compensation. The main provisions in the 1979 Act are:

- s 12 regarding title;
- s 14 regarding quality of goods;
- s 13 regarding sales by description;
- s 15 regarding sales by sample.

It should be noted that the Act also tries to cover business transactions and, therefore, ss 12, 13 and 15 apply to business sales, private sales and business to consumer contracts. Section 14 applies only to sales made in the course of a business. When a sale is made by a private individual, the old rule of *caveat emptor* applies.

Implied conditions under ss 12–15 of the 1979 Act

Section 12 regarding title

Section 12(1) states that there is an implied condition that the seller has a right to sell the goods. If this condition is in breach, that is, the seller is not the owner or otherwise has no right to sell the goods, the true owner will get the goods back and the buyer gets his money back together with appropriate damages. There are, however, some exceptions on which the buyer retains title of the goods.

- *Estoppel (s 21)*

  Where the true owner is aware of the transaction but does not inform the buyer

- *Voidable title (s 23)*

  But it has not been voided at the time of sale and the buyer acts in good faith without knowledge of the defect of the title.

- *Original and subsequent sales (ss 24 and 25)*

  Seller in possession (s 24)

  A seller retains possession after a sale (that is, the original buyer has not taken possession to which he is entitled) and sells to a third party, the third party shall procure a good title.

  Buyer in possession (s 25)

  Similarly, a buyer obtains possession of the goods or document of title before payment and sells on, the third party will have a good title.

- *Factors under the Factors Act 1889*

  Factoring means sales by an agent who is entrusted with the possession of goods to sell in his own name as an apparent owner.

- *Motor vehicle subject to hire purchase*

  When a motor vehicle subject to a hire purchase agreement is sold to a private purchaser as opposed to a business, for example, a garage or a business buying a company car, he will get a good title if he acts in good faith without knowledge of the hire purchase agreement.

Section 14 regarding quality and fitness for purpose

Section 14(2): satisfactory quality

Section 14(2) of the Sale of Goods Act 1979 used to use the term 'merchantable quality'. The Sale and Supply of Goods Act 1994 has rewritten the whole of s 14(2) using the term 'satisfactory quality'. Section 1(1) of the 1994 Act says:

In s 14 of the Sale of Goods Act 1979 (implied terms about quality or fitness) for sub-s (2), there is substituted:

(2) Where the seller sells goods in the course of business, there is an implied term that the goods supplied under the contract are of satisfactory quality.

(2A) For the purposes of this Act, goods are of satisfactory quality if they meet the standard that a reasonable person would regard as satisfactory, taking account of any description of the goods, the price (if relevant) and all the other relevant circumstances.

(2B) For the purposes of this Act, the quality of goods includes their state and condition and the following (among others) are in appropriate cases aspects of the quality of goods:

    (a) fitness for all the purposes for which goods of the kind in question are commonly supplied;

    (b) appearance and finish;

    (c) freedom from minor defects;

    (d) safety; and

    (e) durability.

(2C) The term implied by sub-s (2) above does not extend to any matter making the quality of goods unsatisfactory:

    (a) which is specifically drawn to the buyer's attention before the contract is made;

    (b) where the buyer examines the goods before the contract is made, which that examination ought to reveal; or

    (c) in the case of a contract for sale by sample, which would have been apparent on a reasonable examination of the sample.

The following points should be noted:

- This sub-section only applies to sales in the course of a business. For sales by a private individual, *caveat emptor* applies.

- In the 1979 Act, this was an 'implied *condition*', but here sub-s (2) only says 'implied *term*', which should be interpreted that whether the implied term is a condition or a warranty depends on the circumstances.

- Sub-section (2A) provides that any description of the goods, the price (if relevant) and all other relevant circumstances should be taken into consideration. Therefore, buying a second hand car for £1,000 cannot have similar expectations as buying a brand new top of the range Mercedes.
- Sub-section (2B) spells out that, apart from being fit for all the purposes for which the goods of the kind in question are commonly supplied (for example, a hot water bottle should keep water hot, a freezer should keep food frozen, etc), the goods should be satisfactory in four other aspects as stated in sub-ss (b)–(e). It should also be noted that this is not meant to be an exhaustive list.
- Sub-section (2C) provides some exceptions.

Section 14(3): fitness for the purpose

Section 14(3) of the 1979 Act provides that:

> ... where the seller sells goods in the course of a business and the buyer, expressly or by implication makes known ... to the seller ... any particular purpose for which the goods are being bought, there is an implied term that the goods supplied under the contract are reasonably fit for that purpose, whether or not that is a purpose for which such goods are commonly supplied, except where the circumstances show that the buyer does not rely, or that it is unreasonable for him to rely on the skill or judgment of the seller.

Note: this is an implied term as in s 14(2).

In *Griffiths v Peter Conway Ltd* (1939), Griffiths bought a new tweed coat which gave her a skin irritation. It was held that the coat was fit for normal wear and she had not made it known that she had sensitive skin. In *Grant v Australian Knitting Mills* (1936), there was chemical of sulphite left on the woollen underpants in question and anyone wearing the garment would have suffered from a skin irritation. It was held that the goods were not of merchantable (now 'satisfactory') quality.

Section 13: sale by description

- Sub-section (1) states that, where there is a sale by description, there is an implied term that the goods will correspond with the description.
- Sub-section (2) requires that, if the sale is by sample and description, then goods must correspond with both.

- Sub-section (3) states that goods exposed for sale or hire and selected by the buyer does not prevent a sale is by description. This covers the situation as in *Beale v Taylor* (1967) where a Triumph Herald 1200 car was advertised. The car was inspected and bought by the plaintiff. It was later found that the front was a Triumph 948 welded together with a Triumph 1200 at the back and it was not road worthy. The court held that it was still a sale by description, so the seller was liable.

Note: the term 'goods bought as seen' means that sale by description is excluded.

Section 15: sale by sample
Sub-section (2) provides that, where there is a sale by sample, there is an implied term that:

    (a)   that the bulk will correspond with the sample;

    [(b)   deleted by the Sale and Supply of Goods Act 1994];

    (c)   that the goods will be free from any defect, making their quality unsatisfactory, which would not be apparent on reasonable examination of the sample.

Sub-section (c) covers the situation when the sample is defective itself and such defect is not apparent on reasonable examination, in which case, the seller cannot say that the contract is for the shown and accepted 'defective' goods.

Unfair contract terms in consumer sales

- Contract terms designed to exclude liability for negligence resulting in a consumer's death or personal injury are void.
- A term stating the seller cannot accept liability for any loss or damage (other than death or personal injury) caused by negligence will be subject to a reasonableness test.
- Attempts to exclude liability for breach of contract, or to allow performance of the contract in a way substantially different from what was agreed, is subject to a reasonableness test. For example, a term allowing a travel agent to provide three or four star hotel accommodation when the holiday booked is for a five star hotel is

likely unreasonable and is, therefore, void. If the holidaymaker pays only half the normal price, then it may be reasonable.

The 1977 Act applies to business transactions as well but, in general, it offers higher protection to consumers.

On 1 July 1995, a European Directive came into effect giving further protection to consumers. This Directive has been repealed and replaced by the Unfair Terms in Consumer Contracts Regulations 1999. The Regulations, among other things, state that:

- a contractual term which has not been individually negotiated shall be regarded as unfair if, contrary to the requirement of good faith, it causes a significant imbalance in the parties' rights and obligations arising under the contract to the detriment of the consumer;
- consumer contract must be written in 'plain intelligible language';
- in case of doubt regarding the meaning of a term, it should be construed in favour of the consumer.

Other consumer contracts

The Sale of Goods Act 1979 applies to straightforward contracts in which money changes hands. For contracts such as hire purchase, hire contracts, exchange of goods, contracts for service and contracts for both supply and service, there are other statutes that provide similar protection. These are summarised in the table on the following page.

For example, an engineer is asked to repair the gas boiler in your home. He provides the parts as well as the service to repair the boiler (that is, to identify the problem and put the new parts in). The parts have to be of satisfactory quality under the Supply of Goods and Services Act 1982 (Pt I) s 3 and he has to carry out the work with reasonable care and skill under s 13 of the same Act (Pt II). If the engineer says he has to obtain a part to repair the boiler, but he never comes back for another two to three weeks, he is in breach of s 14 (Pt II). Many times, in a situation like this, there is no agreement on price before the work is completed, in which case, the engineer should and can only charge a reasonable price.

Type of contract	Relevant statute	Equivalent sections
Sale of goods contract	Sale of Goods Act 1979	ss 12, 13, 14
Hire purchase contract	Supply of Goods (Implied Terms) Act 1973	ss 8, 9, 10
Hire contract	Supply of Goods Act 1982 (Pt I)	ss 7, 8, 9 (of course, s 7 talks about a right to bait instead of a right to sell)
Other supply of goods contract, eg, exchange, material and service contract on the material part	Supply of Goods and Services Act 1982 (Pt I)	ss 2, 3, 4
Services rendered in the course of business, eg, pure service contract and material and service contract on the service part	Supply of Goods and Services Act 1982 (Pt II)	Here, we talk about services, so there are no equivalent sections s 13: services have to be provided with reasonable care and skill s 14: if no time is specified, services have to be performed within a reasonable time s 15: if no price agreed, a reasonable price will be paid Note: these sections are terms, not conditions

Contract of employment

Employment contracts are like any other contracts and the general principles of contract law apply. Additionally, there are many statutes which affect the rights, duties and liabilities between employers, employees and their unions. There are no formal requirements for contracts of employment. It can be oral, by contract or in writing. The

Employment Rights Act 1996 though lays down a legal requirement on an employer to give a written statement to an employee who works eight hours or more a week within two months from starting work on the following matters: names of the employer and employee; the date when the employment began; pay; hours of work; holidays; sick pay; pensions; notice for termination; job title; the date of termination for fixed term contract; and disciplinary rules and procedures which apply to the employee. This written statement (or statements) is not the contract itself but the aim of the statutes is to let the employee know where he stands and to provide evidence of the terms and conditions in the case of a dispute.

Duties of employer

There are a number of duties required of employers towards their employees. They include:

- *Duty to pay*

  This is a contractual duty in most cases as well as a common law duty which extends to the situation when there is no work for an employee to do as long as he is ready and willing to work.

- *Duty to provide work*

  This is not an absolute duty but such a duty exists in the following situations:

  (a)   lack of work will deprive the employee from a reasonable income;

  (b)   the reputation of the employee will be affected, for example, a scientist being a pioneer in his field is employed to do nothing; and

  (c)   work is required to maintain and develop the skill of the worker.

- *Duty to indemnify the employee any costs, expenses, losses and liabilities incurred when he is properly performing his duty*

- *Mutual trust and confidence*

  This concerns matters such as oppressive conduct; sexual harassment; verbal or even physical abuse. Failure to observe this duty may lead to an action on contract, tort or unfair dismissal. There is no duty for a former employer to give a reference for an ex-employee, but if one is given, the employer owes a duty of care to the employee not to give an inaccurate or unfair reference.

- *Reasonable care for the safety of employees*

  An employer must provide:

  (a)   safe equipment, plant and premises;

  (b)   safe system of work: examples of this include identifying risk areas, checking them at practicable and regular intervals and preventing long hours of work which may increase risks to and affect the health of the employees;

  (c)   competent and safe co-workers. In *Hudson v Ridge* (1957), the employer was held liable for the injury of his employee who was injured by a co-worker who was a persistent practical joker.

Many statutes have been passed to make breaching these duties a criminal offence. Most of these offences are strict liabilities, so it is not required to prove foreseeability, fault or any other *mens rea* to convict. The major statute in this area is the Health and Safety at Work, etc, Act 1974. Section 2(1) of the Act provides that it shall be the duty of every employer to ensure, so far as is reasonably practicable, the health, safety and welfare at work of all his employers. Section 2(2) provides a non-exhaustive list of matters to which the duty extends:

(a)   plant and systems of work;

(b)   use, handling, storage and transport of articles and substances;

(c)   information, instruction, training and supervision;

(d)   place of work and means of access to and egress from it;

(e)   working environment.

Section 2(3) imposes a duty on employers to issue and revise appropriately a safety policy statement at work.

Sex and racial discrimination at work

It is illegal for an employer to discriminate amongst his employees on the grounds of sex or race. The Race Relations Act 1976 and the Sex Discrimination Act 1975, as amended by the Sex Discrimination (amendment) Act 1986, are written in a similar manner. There are many race related crimes. These Acts only make discrimination unlawful and give individuals the right of direct access to the civil courts and Industrial Tribunals for legal remedies against discrimination. The Acts define discrimination in three main ways:

(a)   direct discrimination;

(b)   indirect discrimination;

(c)   discrimination by means of victimisation.

Direct discrimination

This consists of treating a person less favourably because of his or her sex, race, colour, nationality, ethnic or national origin. In *Coleman v Skyrail Oceanic Ltd* (1981), it was held that the assumption that a husband is normally the breadwinner in the family could amount to sex discrimination. If this assumption is evidenced in an employer's selection for recruits, training, promotion, redundancy or dismissal, the employer can be liable for discrimination.

Indirect discrimination

This is a more difficult concept, which consists of applying a requirement or condition which, intentionally or not, adversely affects one gender or racial group considerably more than another and cannot be justified on non-sexual or racial grounds. In *Hussein v Saintes Complete House Furnishers* (1979), the employers had advertised for a sales assistant who must reside more than five miles from the city centre of Liverpool. This requirement was held to be unlawful indirect discrimination since five miles from the city centre is predominantly white, whereas the city centre had a very high coloured population. Another example of indirect discrimination include the job requirement of an age between 17 and 28 years old because women are less likely to be available for work at this age (*Price v Civil Service Commission* (1978)). Requirements of full time working and even set hours working without justification, which is not difficult to have in these situations, can be discriminatory.

Victimisation

Victimisation arises where a person treats another less favourably than he would treat others because that person has made a complaint or allegation of discrimination or has acted as a witness or informant in connection with proceedings under the Acts or has been involved in another way in their enforcement, or intends to do any of these things.

The Acts provide some exceptions when genuine occupational qualification for a job is proved. Genuine occupational qualification may apply in many situations such as acting, modelling or work in a particular setting where persons of a particular racial group are needed for authenticity. Lastly, it should be noted that these Acts do not only apply to employment but also to many other areas, such as education, the provision of goods, facilities and services.

Termination of employment

Employment contracts are usually terminated with notice. This includes:

(a)   if a contract is a fixed term contract, it ends at the end of the term;

(b)   if it is an indefinite contract or a fixed term contract with a break clause, there may be a period of notice stated in the contract then such notice should be served; and

(c)   if a period of notice is not stated in an indefinite contract, a reasonable period should be given and under no circumstances less than the statutory minimum period of notice.

(d)   redundancies are usually terminations with notice and the employees dismissed are entitled to redundancy payment.

It should be noted that, if a termination is unfair, having adequate notice will not prevent the employee making a claim of unfair dismissal in the Industrial Tribunal (IT). Dismissal without notice is an expression which describes the situations when:

• *The conduct of an employer makes it impossible for an employee to continue working for the organisation*

   Although the person has not been dismissed, he can claim that it is a constructive dismissal on the part of the employer. If he possesses the legal eligibility (that is, he is under normal retirement age, working in Great Britain and has continuous employment for one year), he can file a claim of unfair dismissal within the time limit of three months from the effective date of termination in the IT against his employer.

• *An employer has summarily dismissed an employee*

   If the contractual notice has not been served, it can be a breach of the contract, at times can even be an unfair dismissal. However the dismissal can be lawful if the employee has committed some serious faults in the first place, for example, gross misconduct, dishonesty or incompetence.

• *An employee leaves work and never goes back*

   This, of course, also ends the employment.

5 Tort Law

You should be familiar with the following areas:

- the nature of tortious liability, strict liability and actionable *per se* tort
- liability of an employer for torts committed by employees
- general defences and remedies
- understanding the various concepts in negligence
- various types of trespass and their specific defences and remedies
- nuisance and its comparison with trespass
- defamation, its forms and specific defences

The nature of tortious liability

Torts are civil wrongs other than breach of contract or trust. As with contract, tort is classified as the law of obligation. Contractual obligations arise when an agreement is reached. For tort, there is no term agreed beforehand, however, these are rights, personal or on property, recognised and protected by law. These are our obligations, when living together with others in the society, to take reasonable care and not to intentionally harm others when we conduct our businesses.

Torts include:

- Negligence – carelessness causing physical harm or damage to others.
- Trespass to person – interference with another possibly causing physical harm.
- Defamation – damage to another's reputation.
- Trespass to land/nuisance – interference with another's interest in land.
- Trespass to goods – interference with another's interest in goods.

Other examples of tort include infringements of others' copyrights, patents and other intellectual properties. These are all actions which

79

arise, not from contracts, but from obligations imposed on us by the operation of the law. There are overlaps between tort and crime, for example, assault and battery, both of which are concerned with acts that harm others. One main difference between tort and crime is their objectives. Crimes are conducts which are so undesirable that the law prohibits them. Torts cause damage to others so laws are created to provide compensation to the victims. When a dangerous machine is not fenced, it is a criminal offence. When the machine injures a person, he can sue for compensation.

Liability in tort

For a tortious liability to arise, there must normally be fault on the wrongdoer and damage caused to the claimant.

Fault

A claimant normally has to show the act or omission is committed intentionally, recklessly or negligently. There are, however, exceptions which do not require fault, one being liability under the rule of *Rylands v Fletcher* (1985). The facts of the case were that the defendant contracted to build a reservoir, and the contractor omitted to seal up the existing mine shaft. As a result, the water in the reservoir ran through the shaft and flooded the plaintiff's mine. The House of Lords held that the defendant was liable and the main *ratio* was that:

> A person who, for his own purposes, brings on his lands and collects and keeps there anything likely to do mischief if it escapes must keep it at his peril and, if he does not do so, he is *prima facie* answerable for all the damage which is the natural consequence of its escape.

To summarise, a claimant does not have to prove fault under the rule of *Rylands v Fletcher*; he need only show that there is a thing acummulated which has escaped and caused damage to him. The House of Lords affirmed this principle in many later cases and added that the use of the land by a defendant has to be non-natural. This excludes the ordinary and reasonable use of one's own land or the use that benefits the community. Other types of strict liability are often duties created by statutes (that is, statutory duties); an example is the statutory duty created by the Consumer Protection Act 1987. The Act provides that, as long as a defective goods supplied to a consumer has caused damage to persons or property, the producer is liable to pay compensation. The claimant does not need to prove fault and the absence of negligence or intention is no defence.

Damage

Normally, a claimant must have suffered some physical or financial harm. Again, there are exceptions, namely those crimes which are 'actionable *per se*'. Actionable *per se* means actionable by itself. Examples of this are trespass and libel against which a claimant can obtain relief from the courts without having suffered any actual damage.

Vicarious liability

Vicarious liability is a concept which is quite unique to tort. This is where one person (including legal entities such as a company) can be liable for a tort committed by another. Examples include a principal being liable for its agent; a car owner for another permitted to drive his car and, most importantly, an employer for his employees.

When an employee has committed a tort in the course of his employment, his employer will be liable for those acts which he has authorised to be carried out or for something done incidental to what is authorised. It does not matter whether the authorised act is carried out in a wrongful way. There is no defence, even if the act has been performed in a manner which is expressly forbidden by the employer. In *Limpus v London General Omnibus Company* (1862), the bus company expressly forbade their drivers to race their company buses. The driver in this case did just that and caused damage. The bus company was held to be liable. It has however been said that an employer is not liable if the employee goes on a 'frolic of his own' and leaves his duties to follow a personal pursuit. If the driver in the above case had not done his round, but took the bus down to a nearby seaside for a few hours and carelessly caused an accident during the time, then the employer cannot be held responsible for his action.

It should be noted that the actual wrong doer is also liable. The existence of vicarious liability allows a claimant to sue the employer as well as the employee and, in many cases, the claimant would choose to sue the employers because they usually have more resources to compensate and are covered by insurance. One further point worth mentioning is that vicarious liability does not apply to independent contractors. For example, a main contractor in a construction project is vicariously liable for the torts committed by his own employees. If he employs a sub-contractor to execute certain parts of the work, the sub-contractor generally has to be accountable for his own wrongs occurred when carrying out the work.

The reasons behind employer's vicarious liability are that:

- employees work for their employer and are part of the whole organisation;
- employers are usually in a better financial position to compensate for injuries and are normally covered by insurance;
- the maintenance of safe systems of operation will be encouraged;
- employers will think twice before instructing an employee to commit a dangerous task.

General defences

In this section, we are not discussing the dispute of the facts as a defence (that is, A claims the accident happened in a certain way but B says it did not) nor the remoteness of the damage. Rather, we are discussing some general defences which are legal principle and are available to various torts when appropriate.

Statutory authority

Generally, the rule is that, where a statute gives a power to do something, it is presumed that the power should be exercised carefully. The executor shall not be held liable in tort provided there is no negligence. When a statute orders something to be done, there shall be no liability for performing the duty and for any inevitable consequences.

Consent (*volenti non fit injuria*)

The Latin phrase, *volenti non fit injuria,* means 'there is consent, there is no injury'. The consent can be implied as well as expressed. In sporting events, the competitors cannot sue for trespass to person, even though they have not signed a consent form. The consent has been implied. However, if the act amounts to deliberate or reckless foul play outside the laws of the game, as in *Gilbert v Grundy* (1998), or serious foul play as in *Condon v Basi* (1985), the defendant can be liable.

Knowing the risk does not mean consent. The court will look into the relevant circumstances. In *Dann v Hamilton* (1939), a young lady was injured in a motor accident after having accepted a lift from the driver who she knew had been drinking. She argued that, earlier in the evening, she knew she would be driven by him and at that time the driver was not drunk. It was later that he drank too much and, by then, it was difficult for her to withdraw. Her argument succeeded and she was awarded compensation. Now that drink driving is considered more serious than ever before, it is wondered whether there may be a different decision if a similar case is put forward in court. In *Morris v Murray* (1990), both the plaintiff and defendant were drunk then they decided to go for a ride in a light aircraft and caused the accident. The plaintiff sued, aiming for compensation from the insurance company, but failed. The court held that there was *volenti*.

Another aspect of this defence is concerned with cases brought by rescuers who came to the accident to help but suffered injury themselves. The law generally favours rescuers and the courts will not accept a defence stating that the rescuer has consented to the risk by coming to the accident. In *Haynes v Harwood* (1935), a policeman tried to stop a horse running wild. There was immediate danger to a woman and her children who were nearby. The court held that the defendant was liable to the police and further provided that it is foreseeable that rescuers may come to the scene and will be at risk. The defendant, therefore, normally owes a duty of care to rescuers. This case should be compared with *Cutler v United Dairies Ltd* (1933) where a horse ran away on a quiet country road. The plaintiff volunteered to bring the horse back and by doing so suffered injury. The court did not see any immediate danger and held that the defendant was not liable.

Inevitable accident

When an accident is not intended by the defendant, and could not have been avoided by the exercise of reasonable care, then it is regarded as inevitable accident and no one should be liable for any damages.

Necessity

When an act is necessary to prevent a greater harm or evil, it may be justified. Examples include throwing goods overboard to lighten a ship during a storm which would not be trespass to goods. Normally, a patient signs a consent form before an operation so the surgeon will not be liable for battery. Where emergency medical treatment, not necessarily an operation, is carried out on an unconscious patient, there would not be battery. The court will look into all the circumstances and apply a reasonableness test to decide these cases.

Act of God

In *Nichols v Marland* (1876), a rainstorm which was 'greater and more violent than any within the memory of witnesses' was held to be an act of God and the defendant was found not liable. Although this defence is available, it is rarely used. The defence relies on foreseeability and it is therefore argued that it has no place in a strict liability tort which does not require fault.

Remedies

The most common form of remedy in tort is damages. This is a common law remedy which is usually represented as monetary compensation. The object is to put the claimant back in his original position as if the tort had not been committed so far as money is able to do. This should be compared with the damages awardable in relation to breach of contract, which is to compensate as if the contract is completed. For tort, it is going back to the past and, for contract, it is looking into a hypothetical future. It will be more complex when personal injuries are involved. We live in a capitalist society in which almost everything can be measured in monetary terms. The court will follow previous decisions to assess *quantum*, for example, a broken finger may be £300, a light whiplash may be £500, but a more serious injury needing two months medical attention and causing discomfort for two further years, may be £5,000. There can be many heads of damages such as pain and suffering, loss of amenity, loss of earnings and medical expenses. Regarding extent of damage, the general rule is that damages, which were reasonably foreseeable, are recoverable.

Injunction is an equitable remedy which will be appropriate when damages are not adequate in matters such as threatened or repeated trespass and nuisance. There are other remedies including abatement and forcible ejection. The former is available in nuisance and the latter for trespass to land. Such defences will be discussed in the sections regarding the relevant torts.

Negligence

Negligence in a general sense could mean carelessness causing personal injury, damage to property or financial losses. Contractual obligations have been well established. Students will note that most contract law cases date back to the 19th century. The duty of care in negligence is a relatively new concept. Since the classic case of *Donoghue v Stevenson* (1932), the courts recognise that citizens living amongst each other have a legal duty to take care when they go about their business and to avoid causing harm to others. There is a standard of care we should take and if we fall foul of this generally accepted standard (that is, breach of the duty) and cause damage to another then we are liable to pay compensation. This concept of duty of care is not very different from that of obligation arising from an agreement. Maybe we can say that the courts have 'stolen' the idea in contract to be used in tort.

As mentioned in earlier sections, tort requires fault and harm. The fault elements in negligence are the duty of care and a breach of that duty. A successful claimant in negligence must therefore prove three things:

(a) that the defendant owes him a duty of care;

(b) that the defendant has breached that duty (that is, fallen foul of the standard of care);

(c) that he has suffered damage caused by the breach and are not too remote.

Duty of care

Before the case of *Donoghue v Stevenson* (1932), it was difficult to claim compensation in a civil court without relying on a contract or on other established tort like nuisance and trespass. Mrs Donoghue's friend bought her a bottle of ginger beer and after she drank it she discovered the remnants of a decomposing snail in the bottle. She was ill afterwards. Mrs Donoghue had not bought the beer, so she was not a party to the contract and, therefore, could not sue the manufacturer under contract. She sued for negligence. Lord Atkins in the House of Lords delivered his *ratio* which became the foundation of the law of negligence. He said:

> You must take reasonable care to avoid acts or omissions which you can reasonably foresee would be likely to injure your neighbour. Who, then, in law, is my neighbour? The answer seems to be persons who are so closely and directly affected by my act that I ought reasonably to have them in contemplation as being so affected when I am directing my mind to the acts or omissions which are called in question.

The manufacturer was held to owe its consumer a duty of care and, in breach of this duty and having caused damage, it was liable.

Developments since *Donoghue v Stevenson*

In this section, we look back in time and see how the courts had expanded the law of negligence then later decided that a line had to be drawn somewhere to avoid a possible floodgate problem.

Donoghue was a personal injury case. *Hedley Byrne & Co v Heller & Partners Ltd* (1964) was a case in which an advertising agent asked a bank to give a reference regarding one of their clients and the bank was found to have given a negligent reference. This case extended negligence to pure economic loss suffered because of negligent misstatement. For this type of claim, the law requires a special relationship between the parties, such as professionals like lawyers when advising their clients and possibly big corporations dealing with their small business agents. In *Spartan Steel and Alloys Ltd v Martin & Co* (1973), a contractor negligently cut off the power supply to a steel manufacturer, ruining a whole batch of molten steel. This case distinguished economic losses consequential upon physical damage caused by negligent acts (here, the physical damage of the molten steel and the loss of profit of this batch being the consequential losses) from pure economic loss (the further loss of profit which would have occurred if there was no power cut). The court held that the defendant was liable to the consequential losses but not for the pure economic loss. Later, in *Anns v London Borough of Merton* (1978), Anns bought a house and later discovered the foundation was defective. The plaintiff claimed that the council should have spotted the defect when the house was being built and succeeded. This case changed the position as set out in *Spartan Steel* and took negligence into the area of pure economic loss caused by negligent acts or omissions. We can also see from this case the courts' readiness to expend the liability situation under negligence at the time. It was pure economic loss in the sense that there was no personal injury and no damage to other property except the house was defective itself. Since *Anns*, there was considerable expansion in the duty of care situations and, consequently, the courts felt that it could have gone too far which might result in everybody suing everybody else. In *Governors of the Peabody Donation Fund v Sir Lindsay Parkinson* (1985), although the House of Lords had not disapproved of the principle laid down in *Anns*, it had added that it had to be 'just and reasonable' for a duty of care to exist.

Further retreat from *Anns* was evidenced in a Hong Kong case, *Yuen Kun Yeu v Attorney General for Hong Kong* (1987). Lord Keith in the Privy Council advocated that:

(a)   foreseeability was necessary but not sufficient;

(b)   a relationship of 'proximity' between the parties was also required;

(c)   it had to be just and reasonable to impose a duty of care.

These are the general principles adopted in recent negligence cases. Finally, in 1990, *Anns* had been expressly overruled in the House of Lords' case of *Murphy v Brentwood District Council* (1990). Whereas economic loss caused by negligent misstatement is still recoverable under *Hedley Byrne v Heller*, economic loss caused by negligent act or omission is no longer claimable.

One last paragraph here will hopefully make the concept of negligence absolutely clear. One of the most common examples in negligence is the motor accident. It is foreseeable that careless driving will cause personal injuries and damage to properties, therefore, drivers owe other road users a duty of care. It is just and reasonable that such a legal duty is imposed. If a driver drives negligently (that is, his standard of care falls foul of an acceptable standard) and causes damages to others, he is liable. It is also possible that he has committed a traffic offence. The very same formula applies:

(a)   duty of care;

(b)   breach of the duty;

(c)   damage caused which is not too remote.

Nervous shock

We have discussed the situations when personal injury, damage to property and pure economic loss caused by negligent statements are foreseeable, the law imposes a duty of care on the defendant. In this section, we shall discuss a more complex type of loss, that is, nervous shock. Is it just and reasonable to impose a duty on citizens to avoid causing nervous shock in others? Can nervous shock of another be foreseeable? The cases relating to nervous shock will also give an insight of how negligent cases have developed and are decided.

Nervous shock can now be regarded as identifiable psychiatric illnesses. In the past, it was not as easy to identify this medical problem and, therefore, the courts were reluctant to award damages relating to nervous shock. In *Bourhill v Young* (1943) (some 10 years after *Donoghue v Stevenson*), a motor cyclist was fatally injured in an accident. A pregnant lady from a distance of about 15 yards saw the accident and suffered shock leading to her miscarriage. She made a claim and the court held that she was not owed a duty of care because it was not reasonably foreseeable that someone might suffer from shock. In *King v Phillips* (1953), a mother heard her child screaming and saw his tricycle go under a taxi. He was not hurt. The mother's claim of nervous shock was not successful.

Some 30 years after *Donoghue*, in *Boardman v Sanderson* (1964), the defendant negligently reversed his car and injured the plaintiff's son. The plaintiff witnessed the incident and suffered shock. The issue of nervous shock was brought before the court (the insurance company would have paid for the personal injury suffered by the son already) which held that the defendant was aware that the plaintiff was nearby therefore owed a duty of care to her. Then came the milestone case of *McLoughlin v O'Brian* (1982) where there was a serious road accident. The plaintiff's husband and daughters were badly injured. She visited them in hospital and suffered shock. It was held in the House of Lords that the defendant owes the plaintiff a duty of care because it was reasonably foreseeable that close relatives would come upon the aftermath. It further added that distance and time should be considered. The Hillsborough FA Cup disaster case, *Alcock v Chief Constable of South Yorkshire Police* (1991), was a civil action brought by a group of claimants. The main issue of the case was not to decide whether the police were negligent. They were, and those who died or sustained injuries during the accident had been paid compensation already. The main question here was: what about those relatives who suffered shock from watching the live television broadcast or from attending the mortuary?

The court held that:

(a) Simultaneous television is equivalent to being within the sight and hearing of the event. Duties of care were owed to those who could recognise their close relatives from the television, excluding those whose relatives were not recognisable from the claim. Close relatives include parents and spouse relationships. For fiancée or grandparents, the courts required some exceptional circumstances, such as proven love, affection and care, on a case by case basis in order to allow a claim.

(b) Attending the mortuary more than eight hours after the incident was outside the scope of immediate aftermath.

Some may find the latter point to be peculiar. The answer could be that a line has to be drawn somewhere.

Breach of duty

Here, a claimant has to prove that the defendant has fallen foul of a standard which is expected from a reasonable person. This is called the 'reasonable man test'. To decide what is reasonable, the court will consider:

- *How much risk is involved?*

    If it is high risk, a reasonable person would have taken more precautions to prevent any accident (*Hilder v Associate Partland Cement Ltd* (1961) as compared to *Bolton v Stone* (1951)).

- *Would the consequences be serious should the risk materialise?*

    In *Paris v Stepney BC* (1951), a council worker had sight only in one eye. He was not provided with safety goggles which were not usually required for the kind of job involved. The court considered the seriousness of the risk (total blindness) and the simple precaution which could have been taken and held that the council had not taken reasonable care and was, therefore, liable.

- *The practicability of the precautions*

    There may be precautions which can be taken but, if they are not practical to take, the accident may be just a pure accident and no one is legally liable. Again, the reasonable man test is applied to decide whether the precautions are practicable or otherwise.

- *Special skill*

    The standard of care expected from a professional or skilled person is that of a reasonable person possessing the professional or special skill. Therefore, a lawyer and accountant are measured by the standards expected from a reasonable lawyer and accountant. Further, learner drivers, trainee doctors and nurses are legally measured by the standards of a reasonable driver, qualified doctor or nurse. This rule prevents institutions using personnel on training to execute risky tasks and if they are used they should be supervised.

Causation and remoteness of damage

The last hurdle for a claimant is to prove that the damage suffered was caused by the defendant and that it was not too remote.

Causation

This is concerned with the issue of whether, as a matter of fact, the damage was caused by the negligent act. If there could only be one cause, the so called 'but for test' will be applied. If the harm would not have occurred but for the defendant's breach of duty, the defendant is liable. In *Barnett v Chelsea and Kensington Hospital Management Committee* (1969), a doctor in the defendant's hospital sent the plaintiff's husband away telling him to see his own doctor. The patient died from arsenic poisoning five hours later. Although it was clear that the doctor was negligent, the court held that he was not liable for the death because the medical reports showed that the patient was beyond help and would have died in any event. It is not always possible to give a 'yes' or 'no' answer to the but for test. In *McGhee v National Coal Board* (1973), the plaintiff contracted dermatitis after cleaning out the defendant's brick kilns. It could not be sure if the defendant actually caused the illness suffered, but it was found that no washing facilities were provided for the plaintiff who had to return home unwashed. Further expert evidence showed that the absence of washing facilities materially increased the risk of injury. The defendant was found liable.

When there are a number of possible causes, the court would require a claimant to establish, on a balance of probability, that the defendant's breach of duty was the cause of the damage. It gets more complicated when there are successive causes. As, and only as, a general principle, the first and subsequent causes bring about the same damage, then only the first defendant is liable. In *Performance Cars Ltd v Abraham* (1962), it was found that the second defendant's car negligently collided with the plaintiff's but the second defendant was not liable to pay for the cost of a re-spray because the plaintiff's car was damaged by the first defendant's car already and would require re-spraying anyway. If the subsequent breach has caused increased damage, the subsequent defendant generally (but not always) is only liable for the damage reduced by the damage already caused by the first defendant. If the damages caused by the second defendant in the *Performance Cars* case above required the replacements of a head light and the front bumper, as well as the re-spraying, the second defendant should be liable to pay for the head light and the bumper but not the re-spray. If the subsequent cause is a natural event, the defendant's liability should be restricted up to the occurrence of the natural event. In *Jobling v Associated Dairies Ltd* (1982), the plaintiff's back was injured due to the negligence of the defendant. Before the trial, he was found to have a spinal disease unrelated to the injury which rendered him totally unfit for work. The court held that the defendant was only liable up to the onset of the spinal disease.

Remoteness of damage

After causation is established, a claimant may sometimes still be denied any compensation on the ground that the damage is regarded to be too remote. Before we discuss in detail what 'remoteness of damage' means, we shall refer to a few wise words expressed by Lord Denning in *Lamb v Camden London Borough Council* (1981):

> The truth is that all these three: duty, remoteness and causation, are all devices by which the courts limit the range of liability for negligence or nuisance ... Sometimes, it is done by limiting the range of the persons to whom duty is owed. Sometimes, it is done by saying that there is a break in the chain of causation. At other times, it is done by saying the consequence is too remote to be a head of damage. All these devices are useful in their way. But, ultimately, it is a question of policy for the judges to decide.

It should be understood that not every wrongful act, which causes harm, is subject to compensation. Sometimes, an injured party has to accept that his case was a pure accident and that nobody is liable. The law has to draw a line somewhere, otherwise we may end up in a society where everybody is suing everybody else. If this is understood, there should be less confusion in studying this area of law.

Throughout the years, the courts have developed some principles regarding remoteness, the first being the use of the 'foreseeable consequence test'. In *The Wagon Mound (No 1)* (1961), a ship negligently discharged fuel oil into Sydney Harbour. The facts found were that a piece of cotton waste was floating on the oil which was set alight by sparks from nearby welding. The fire damaged a wharf. The Privy Council held that the defendants were liable for the fouling but not for the fire damage. The *ratio* was that the type of damage which is subject to compensation should be reasonably foreseeable by a defendant when he acted carelessly. In *Doughty v Turner Manufacturing Co Ltd* (1964), an asbestos cement cover was dropped into some molten liquid. An explosion followed and the plaintiff was injured. It was held that the splash could be foreseeable but not the explosion and, therefore, the defendant was not liable. Further rules established are that, as long as the type of damage is reasonably foreseeable, it does not matter how it came about and the extent of the damage is more than it could have been foreseen.

Res ipsa loquitur

Res ipsa loquitur is a Latin phrase which means 'the thing speaks for itself'. Generally, a claimant has to prove that the defendant is negligent. However, there are circumstances in which a claimant cannot show how the accident actually came about, for example, the claimant was under an anaesthetic during an operation, then *res ipsa loquitur* may be invoked to help him. All he needs to prove is:

(a) that the thing causing the damage is under the defendant's exclusive control;

(b) that the accident could not have happened in the absence of negligence.

If the court accepts these, then the burden of proof will shift to the defendant, who has to prove that he was not negligent. Examples of situations where defendants have been found liable under *res ipsa loquitur* include swabs being left in a patient's body after an operation (*Martin v Osborne* (1939)) and a plaintiff being struck by an object falling from the defendant's premises.

Contributory negligence

The old common law rule on contributory negligence was strict. If a claimant's injury was caused partly by his own fault, no matter how small and insignificant it was, he could not recover anything. The Law Reform (Contributory Negligence) Act 1945 has changed this position. Section 1(1) provides that:

> Where any person suffers damage as the result partly of his own fault and partly the fault of another person or persons, a claim in respect of that damage shall not be defeated by reason of the fault of the person suffering the damage, but the damages recoverable in respect thereof shall be reduced to such extent as the court thinks just and equitable having regard to the claimant's share in the responsibility for the damage.

In *Sayers v Harlow Urban District Council* (1958), the plaintiff was locked in a public toilet because of a faulty lock. She needed to catch a bus, so stepped on the toilet roll in order to climb out but injured herself in the process. The court held that the council was negligent, but reduced the damage recoverable by 25%. In *Froom v Butcher* (1976), the defendant was found to have driven negligently, but the damage was reduced by 25% because the plaintiff was not wearing a seat belt which would have prevented the injury altogether. The court also provided *obiter dicta* that, if the injury would have been less severe, then the reduction should be 15%. If the injury would have been the same, even if a seat belt had been worn, then there should be no reduction. Later cases confirmed these *obiter dicta*, which has survived the enactment of the compulsory wearing of seat belts. In *Capps v Miller* (1989), the damage was reduced by 10% for the motor cyclist's failure to fasten his crash helmet. It was also said that failure to wear a helmet would merit a higher percentage of reduction.

A very young child cannot be held to be contributory negligent. For an older child, a judge should consider whether he or she is of such an age as can be reasonably expected to take precautions for his or her own safety (*Gough v Thorne* (1966)). Some allowances should also be given to the infirm, for example, elderly pedestrians crossing the road. Finally, rescuers and workmen suing their employer for breach of statutory regulations are rarely held to be contributory negligent.

Occupiers' liability for dangerous premises

The Occupiers' Liability Act 1957

Section 2(1) of the Occupiers' Liability Act 1957 provides that an occupier owes a single 'common duty of care' to all his visitors. Section 2(2) further provides that the duty of care is to take such care as in all the circumstances of the case is reasonable to see that the visitor will be reasonably safe in using the premises. Under the common law rules, occupiers are those who have occupational control over the premises. Therefore, landlords who have let premises to a tenant and parted with possession are not usually occupiers for the purpose of the Act. However, they may still be liable under common law negligence and the Defective Premises Act 1972. Visitors include those who have the occupier's express or implied permission to enter the premises. The 1957 Act does not cover trespassers to whom some protection is offered by the Occupiers' Liability Act 1984. It is also generally accepted that the duty applies only to damages caused by the condition of the premises or land itself but not the activities carried out there. For the latter, it is subject to the common law. The standard of care is the same as that in an ordinary action in negligence (that is, reasonable man test) and the factors to be considered are also the same (see 'Breach of duty', above).

Section 2(3) of the 1957 Act provides that an occupier must be prepared for children to be less careful than adults. Therefore, if the occupier expects children to enter his premises (private premises as well as public parks and playgrounds), then those premises must be safe for their use.

An occupier may discharge his duty under this Act by giving a warning of the danger (for example, a warning sign) but the warning is not to be treated without more as absolving the occupier from liability, unless in all the circumstances it was enough to enable the visitor to be reasonably safe (s 2(4)(a) of the 1957 Act). Therefore, a warning does not automatically discharge the duty. Obviously, a sign at a hidden corner will not suffice. If the nature of the risk is obvious, a simple 'Danger' sign may help the occupier; if otherwise, an occupier should indicate the nature and location of the danger to enable the visitor to avoid it (*Roles v Nathan* (1963)). In some cases, a physical barrier may be required. A sign 'Enter at your own risk' does not attempt to discharge the occupier's duty, but to raise the defence of *volenti non fit injuria* (see above).

Occupiers' liability to trespassers

Trespassers are those persons who intentionally enter onto others' land without lawful permission or remain on the land after permission has been withdrawn. Permission (or 'licence') can be expressed or implied. Common law is generally hostile to trespassers and the Occupiers' Liability Act 1957 has not covered trespassers as visitors. The Occupiers' Liability Act 1984 extends and provides a duty of care owed to 'persons other than his visitors'. Section 1(3) of the 1984 Act stipulates that the occupier owes the duty of care if:

(a) he is aware of the danger or has reasonable grounds to believe that it exists;

(b) he knows or has reasonable grounds to believe that there are others in the vicinity of the danger concerned or that he may come into the vicinity of the danger; and

(c) the risk is one against which, in all the circumstances of the case, he may reasonably be expected to offer the others some protection.

Section 1(4) provides that the standard of care is 'such care as is reasonable in all circumstances'. This is an objective standard of reasonable care. The court will look into all relevant circumstances such as the nature and character of the entry, the age of the entrant, the nature of the premises and the extent of the risk. Section 1(5) provides that, when appropriate, an occupier may discharge his duty by taking reasonable steps to give a warning of the danger concerned or to discourage persons from incurring the risk. Section 1(6) provides that *volenti* is a defence and, therefore, an obvious sign of 'Enter at your own risk' will probably help an occupier defending against an action brought by a trespasser than a visitor. One last point to note is that an occupier can only be liable for the death or personal injury of a trespasser, but not for damage to property under the 1984 Act, while a person can be liable for damage to property of a visitor as well under the 1957 Act.

Trespass

Trespass is the oldest tort. It is a tort which is actionable *per se* (meaning actionable by itself). There is no need for a claimant to suffer any damages before he can sue. There are three categories of trespass: trespass to land, to person and to goods. We shall now discuss each of them.

Trespass to land

Trespass to land is the intentional entering into another person's land without lawful permission or remaining on the land after the permission has been withdrawn. Placing a chattel (a legal term for movable things) on another's land is also a trespass. Therefore, a person may have permission to enter the premises in the first place, but once the permission is withdrawn and he remains on the land, then he will be liable for trespass. Tunnelling underground and protruding above another's land are also trespass. In *Kelson v Imperial Tobacco Company* (1957), the defendant was liable for trespass by protruding a sign over the plaintiff's land. The Civil Aviation Act 1982 provides that aircraft flying at a reasonable height cannot be trespass, though the Act also makes those who fly the aircraft strictly liable for any damage they cause.

There are a few specific defences available for trespass to land

- *Express or implied licence*

  'Licence' is a legal term meaning permission, which can be expressed or implied. Implied permission includes allowing sales persons and canvassers to walk up your garden path to your front door. When you have a sticker on your door saying 'No salespersons' or 'No canvassers' or when you ask them to leave and they refuse, then it has become a trespass.

- *Authorised or justified by law*

  One example of a defence for trespass to land is a bailiff when executing a court order. Another example is the police having powers conferred to them by the Police and Criminal Evidence Act 1984 to enter premises and search them under certain circumstances.

- *Necessity*

  This includes a land block situation where a piece of land cannot be reached without crossing the land of another. This may sometimes create a right of way under land law. Another situation is when a person has to make an entrance to retake or retain possession of his own property. Of course, the exercise of this right must be reasonable. In *Rigby v Chief Constable of Northampton* (1985), it was held that necessity was a defence, provided that there was no fault on the part of the defendant in contributing to the state of the necessity.

- *Involuntary entry*

  The basis of this defence is the lack of intention, for example, landing in a parachute.

Remedies

- *Damages*

  In trespass cases, the damages are often trivial. If the use of the land by a defendant has some commercial value, damages such as the letting value may be awarded. In many cases, the court may award only nominal damages which might be as low as one pence. This is sometimes significant because, generally, the loser of a case will be ordered to pay the legal costs of the winner. Such costs may not be the full sum of the lawyer's bill but will, at least, cover part of it. If some damage has been incurred, the court will usually award damages measured by the diminution in value of the land rather than the cost of restoration.

- *Injunction*

  A claimant may seek an injunction order in cases of threatened or continuing trespass.

- *Ejection*

  A person who has been dispossessed may bring an action for ejection where he can establish his right of possession and recovery of land.

- Mesne *profits*

  This represents a claimant's loss relating to the land in question during the period that he has been dispossessed. This includes the value of the use and occupation of the land, any damage to the land itself and the reasonable costs of regaining possession.

- *Distress damage feasant*

  Where damage has been caused by a chattel trespass, the claimant may retain the chattel until the damage has been paid for.

- *Expulsion*

  This may be the most commonly used self-help remedy. It was established in *Collins v Renison* (1754) that a person in possession is entitled to use reasonable force to expel a trespasser provided he has first asked the person to leave.

Trespass to person

There are three forms of trespass to person: assault, battery and false imprisonment.

Assault and battery

'An assault is an act which causes another person to apprehend the infliction of immediate, unlawful force on his person; a battery is the actual infliction of unlawful force on another person' (*Collins v Wilcock* (1984)). It is generally accepted that words alone, without some form of action, cannot be assault but this is not without any exception because of some recent conflicting decisions. For assault, there must be fear. Hitting someone on the back is a battery without an assault because there is no fear apprehended. A misplaced punch is an assault without battery. No one may touch another without his or her consent or some lawful justification. Any contact, however trivial, is sufficient force for battery. In *Collins v Wilcock* (1984), an unwanted kiss was held to be battery. Indirect touching is also sufficient, for example, to throw a stone hitting a person.

It is clear that the defendant must have intended to commit the act that constitutes the trespass. Possibly, recklessness will suffice. It is however not as straight forward to answer whether the intention has to be hostile. Traditionally, the answer was negative. In *Cole v Turner* (1704), as little as the mere touching of another in anger was held to be battery. *Collins v Wilcock* (1984) set out that the tort of trespass protects persons, not only from physical injury, but also safeguards their personal dignity from any form of physical molestation. However, in *Wilson v Pringle* (1986), the defendant pulled the plaintiff's school bag from his shoulder as a practical joke and caused injury to the plaintiff. It was held that 'touching must be proved to be hostile touching'. Indeed, there are many forms of contact which are unavoidable and are generally accepted as consequences of social intercourse, for example, touching a person on the shoulder to attract his attention. There is no hostile intention, probably the opposite. These contacts, if kept within reasonable bounds, are acceptable. Maybe the best answer to the issue discussed in this paragraph is that it depends on the circumstances in each case.

False imprisonment

False imprisonment is 'the unlawful imposition of constraint on another's freedom of movement from a particular place' (*Collins v Wilcock* (1984)). Unlawful arrests are usually false imprisonment. The tort does not require physically locking someone up. Compelling a person to remain in an open field by threatening him with a shotgun will suffice. When the restraint is lawful, it will be a total defence. It is lawful for a shop detective to detain a person who has shoplifted for the police to take him away. It would be different if the person is detained without having stolen goods found on him or the detention has been for an unreasonable length of time (*John Lewis & Co Ltd v Tims* (1952)).

The restraint has to be total. In *Bird v Jones* (1845), the usual footway on Hammersmith Bridge was fenced off for viewing a regatta on the river. The plaintiff insisted on crossing the footway and climbed over the fence but was restrained by the clerk of the bridge who, together with two policemen, managed to prevent him from going any further and told him that he could go back and take an alternative route. However, the plaintiff remained there for over half an hour and then tried to force his way through. He was then taken into custody for assaulting the police. The court held that there was no false imprisonment because there was no total restraint of the plaintiff's liberty. He could have gone back the way he came.

Specific defences for trespass to person

Other general defences such as *volenti* are available when appropriate. In this section, we discuss a few specific defences:

- parental authorities are available for parents disciplining their children. Quasi-parental authorities are available, for example, when teachers exercise their authority appropriately to keep control over their pupils;
- using force or detaining someone within a justifiable length of time on the basis of self-defence is lawful. It must be noted that the force used must be reasonable;
- it has been mentioned earlier that statutory or judicial authority such as a lawful arrest is also a defence.

Trespass to goods (or chattels)

This area of law is now covered by the Torts (Interference with Goods) Act 1977 as well as by the common law. Trespass to goods is an intentional, unjustifiable and direct interference with the claimant's possession of goods or the carrying out of an unjustifiable act denying a person of his legal right to possess the goods. The latter is sometimes called 'conversion'. This includes taking goods, moving goods from one place to another and touching the goods, causing damage. Other examples include striking a person's dog and erasing a tape recording without consent of the owner.

Nuisance

Nuisance is divided into private nuisance and public nuisance. Although they are both classified as nuisance, the nature of each is quite distinct. Private nuisance protects people from unjustifiable interference of the use of their land from their neighbours and they are civil actions between adjacent landowners and occupiers. Public nuisance is a crime which protects certain public rights, mainly the right to an unobstructed and safe use of public areas. It is also actionable in tort if an individual has suffered more than the public generally.

Private nuisance

A generally accepted judicial definition of private nuisance is 'an unlawful interference with a person's use or enjoyment of land or some right, or in connection with it'. Private nuisance operates between adjacent landowners and occupiers and, therefore, only the occupier and the landlord of the adjacent land, together with the person who created the nuisance in the adjacent land, can be jointly and severally liable. It protects interests in land and, therefore, only the owner or occupier with an interest in the land affected can sue. In *Malone v Laskey* (1907), it was held that even the wife of the tenant would not have a right of action in nuisance. The nuisance operates against a general state of affairs rather than one isolated incident. An isolated bonfire in one's garden or an all night noisy party will not be nuisance though other actions such as negligence if any damage has been incurred and complaints to the Environment Department and police can be taken. Examples of private nuisance include: tree branches and roots encroaching on the neighbours land; the collapse of neighbouring buildings; the use of premises as a brothel or a sex shop; a recurrence of noxious fumes, smells, dust, vibration and noise.

Private nuisance must be an unreasonable use of the defendant's land. The court will also take into consideration the locality as well. In *Sturges v Bridgman* (1879), it was expressed 'what would be a nuisance in Belgrave Square would not necessarily be so in Bermondsy'. However, another *ratio* in the case was that there is no defence saying that the claimant comes to the nuisance. It appears that the main thing the court will look into is the interference itself. If the claimant or his property is abnormally sensitive, his nuisance action may fail. In *Robson v Kilvert* (1889), the plaintiff complained about the heat from the manufacturing process from his neighbour downstairs damaging his paper stock. The court found that ordinary paper would not have the same problem and concluded that the plaintiff was carrying on an exceptionally delicate trade and the defendant's activity was perfectly lawful. The defendant was not liable. Sometimes, the court will also consider the motive of the action complained. In *Christie v Davey*

(1893), a wood carver who did not like music, made a lot of noise by blowing a whistle, knocking on trays and shouting when his neighbour was having piano lessons. The court held that the neighbour's use of their property was reasonable but his malice (the motive) was not.

Nuisance is not actionable *per se*. Usually, damage has to be proven. There are three possible remedies which can be sought against nuisance: damages, injunction and a form of self-help known as abatement. Damages are monetary compensation for physical damage. This could also cover non-physical losses such as personal discomfort and inconvenience. Injunction is appropriate where the nuisance is continuing. Abatement is the removal of the nuisance by the victim himself. Though it is available, the law does not encourage it. If a situation is not as straightforward as cutting branches from overhanging trees, there could be complications. If entry to another's land is required, notice must be given or the abator will be a trespasser.

Other general defences, for example, statutory authority, may be available for nuisance. There are also defences specific to private nuisance such as prescription. If a private nuisance has continued and has been actionable for 20 years, the defendant may have gained a prescriptive right to commit the nuisance. This rule, however, is not absolute and is subject to reasonableness. Reasonable use of one's own property is another specific defence (see *Christie v Davey* (1893), above).

Comparison between private nuisance and trespass to land

The table overleaf sets out the comparison between the two torts:

Private nuisance	Trespass to land
The matter complained about is a state of affairs and is repetitive	One act of trespass will suffice
Nuisance does not require entry	Trespass requires entry to land
Indirect interference is sufficient, for example, smell, noise, etc	This relates to direct infringement of one's interests
Damage must be proven so this is not actionable *per se*	This is a tort which is actionable *per se*

Public nuisance

Public nuisance is a crime which may be defined as an unlawful act or omission which obstructs or causes damage or inconvenience to the public. Actions are usually prosecuted by the Attorney General or his representative. The place affected is not a private place but a public area. In the past, public nuisance covered four main areas: public decency, public health, public convenience and public safety. The former two are now largely subject to legislative regulations. The latter two play the major part in modern public nuisance cases which include causing obstruction and dangers to the highway or public areas.

When an individual has suffered more than the public has, he is generally entitled to bring an action in tort. In *Castle v St Augustines Links Ltd* (1922), golf balls were driven out frequently onto the public highway and on this occasion smashed a taxi's windscreen and injured the driver. This was a public nuisance matter. Further, the driver also sued for negligence and successfully obtained damages.

Defamation

What is defamation?

Defamation can be defined as 'the publication of a false statement which reflects [badly] on the reputation of the person defamed, lowering him in the estimation of right thinking members of society, making them shun or avoid him or regard him with feelings of hatred, ridicule or contempt'. The claimant must prove that:

The publication is a false statement

It is an absolute defence if the statement is true however much it damages the reputation of a person. It is also a defence if the statement is substantially true. If A tells others that B owes him £1,000 when it is actually only £960, B cannot sue for defamation because the statement, although not absolutely true, is substantially true. It may be different if the actual figure was £100.

The material has been published to a third party

Publication in defamation means communication to a third party. The tort protects a claimant's reputation in the eyes of others not his personal feelings, therefore communication made to the claimant alone, however untrue and insulting, is not defamation. Thus, communication to the defendant's spouse does not constitute publication for the Bible states that, when two persons marry, they become one (*Wennhak v Morgan* (1888)). Indeed, husband and wife do talk about anything and everything. Communication to a claimant's spouse is publication (*Wenman v Ash* (1853)). The publication has to be intended or reasonably anticipated by the defendant. Speaking loudly to another whilst being overheard by a third party can be actionable. However, abuses spoken in the heat of an argument, which are intended and understood by others to be mere insults, are normally not defamatory (*Parkins v Scott* (1862)). Leaving documents where others might read them can be publication. A letter addressed to a particular person is supposed to be published to the addressee but in some situations the sender should anticipate that a third party (for example, a clerk in the office or a spouse) may read the letter and should take care what is written. Marking 'private' or 'private and confidential' on correspondence may help the sender. Presumably postcards, telegrams and fax transmissions are deemed published to those who may easily read the contents such as postal officials, the recipient's family or colleagues at work. It is now common practice for the first cover page of a fax transmission to include a statement stating that the contents are intended to be read and used by the addressee only.

Each fresh publication, even though it states the same thing, is actionable each time. It is no defence for C to say that it was true that A told him B owed A £1,000. This area of law is particularly relevant to publishers. Where a book, newspaper or a journal contains defamatory materials, the author, the publisher and the printer can all be liable. Other parties down the chain such as booksellers, news vendors and even librarians can also be liable. They will, however, have a defence if they can show that they had no knowledge or ought not to have given rise to a suspicion that the material was defamatory and their lack of knowledge was not due to negligence. The Defamation Act 1996 created a new statutory defence which extends this common law defence of innocent dissemination to secondary publishers such as printers, broadcasters of live television programmes, communication network service operators and computer systems providers. In order to plead this defence, they have to show that they had no reason to know or believe that the publication was defamatory and had taken reasonable care in relation to the publication.

The statement tends to lower the claimant's reputation in the estimation of right thinking members of society

If A tells others that B was raped which is not true, A may be morally wrong but he is still not liable for defamation because right thinking members of society would not shun or avoid a rape victim nor regard B with feelings of hatred, ridicule or contempt. In *Byrne v Dean* (1937), after an illegal gaming machine in a golf club was removed by the police, a note was put on the club's notice board saying that Byrne had informed the police. This was found to be untrue but the defendant was not liable because right thinking members of the society would have approved the action of informing the police.

The statement refers to the claimant

The defamatory statement must refer to the claimant, who does not have to be named. As long as an ordinary sensible reader would understand the words as referring to the claimant in the light of some special facts, it will be sufficient. Generally, defamation of a class of persons is not actionable. No accountant can sue for statements such as 'all accountants are thieves' or ' I know an accountant in this office who steals money'. If the reference is to a limited class or group then it is possible that all members in the group can sue. For the above statement, which refers to an accountant in the office, if the firm consists of only two to three accountants then all of them would be able to sue. The court will also consider the generality of the charge and the extravagance of the accusation (*Knupffer v London Express Newspaper Ltd* (1944)).

Two forms of defamation

Libel is a defamatory statement made in permanent form while slander is made in transitory form. Written or printed statements are libel, as are caricatures, drawings, motion pictures and many others. Section 16 of the Defamation Act 1952 provides that defamatory broadcastings on radio and television are libel, not slander. Defamation made by speech or gesture is slander. It is important to distinguish between the two because libel is actionable *per se* (that is, there is no need to prove financial loss) but slander is not, except when it is concerned with:

(a) committing a crime which is punishable by imprisonment;

(b) transmitting a contagious disease, rendering the person so infected that he is liable to be excluded from society (for example, leprosy and venereal disease);

(c) unchastity in a woman;

(d) unfitness for any office, profession, calling, trade or business held or carried on by the claimant at the time of the publication (Defamation Act 1952).

Innuendo

Some words are self-evidently defamatory. Innuendo is defamation by implication though the material on the face of it does not appear to be defamatory in its ordinary sense. In *Cassidy v Daily Mirror Newspapers Ltd* (1929), the defendants published in their newspaper a picture of the plaintiff's husband with another lady announcing that they had been engaged. Mrs Cassidy claimed that the material imputed by innuendo that she was immorally cohabiting with a man. She won her case. In *Tolley v Fry* (1931), the defendant, a chocolate manufacturer, published an advertisement without the consent of the plaintiff, an amateur golfer, showing a picture of him with a packet of the defendant's chocolate. The court agreed with the plaintiff that his name and amateur status had been prostituted.

Specific defences

Justification
This covers the situations when the statements are true or substantially true.

Fair comment
This defence is restricted to fair comment on a matter of public interest which includes subjects relating to the behaviour of public figures such as politicians, government and other public officials. Things like works of art, books, plays, public exhibitions, newspapers and broadcasts are presumed to be submitted for public criticism and, therefore, are also subject to this defence. The comment has to be honest, relevant and free from malice or improper motive. The statement must consist of opinion or comment and not of fact.

Privilege
There are occasions which are said to be absolutely privileged. Defamatory statements made during these occasions are not actionable. There are also qualified privileged situations, in which the defence will be defeated if the claimant can prove that the defendant has acted from malice or that he abused the occasion for an improper purpose.

Absolute privilege

Parliamentary proceedings
Statements made during the course of parliament proceedings such as debates in the parliament and proceedings in committees attract absolute privilege against defamation action (Bill of Rights 1688). This also covers officially authorised parliamentary reports and other papers as well. Extracts of these only attract qualified privilege.

Judicial proceedings
Statements made in the ordinary course of court or tribunal proceedings are absolutely privileged. Professional communications between solicitors, barristers and their clients also attract absolute privilege.

Official communications

Communications between one Officer of State and another in the course of their duty attract absolute privilege. Officers of State are Ministers and Secretaries of State. Communications between lower rank officials are only covered by qualified privilege.

Qualified privilege

- Statements where the maker has a duty, either legally or morally, to inform another for the protection of an interest, and the receiver has a duty or interest to receive the information, attract qualified privilege. When a director reports to the board of an employee's misbehaviour, he cannot be sued even when the statements are defamatory. But if the claimant can prove malice or improper motive, then the director will be liable.

- Statements in protection of one's private interests and letter of complaint or report to a proper authority are also privileged.

- Fair and accurate reports of parliamentary and public judicial proceedings attract qualified privilege. These reports are not the absolute privileged ones which are directly authorised by Parliament and the courts.

- Fair and accurate reports of various matters of public interest and importance such as the proceedings of the United Nations, the International Court of Justice and public meetings of local authorities are privileged.

The defence under the Defamation Act 1996

The Act provides a defence to those distributors, not an author, editor or publisher, who has taken reasonable care in relation to the publication if he neither knew or ought to have known that the contents were defamatory. Section 2 of the Act further provides that a defendant can make an offer to make amends, that is, to correct the statement, apologise and pay agreed or determined damages. Such an offer can later be a complete defence in the court if the defendant has innocently defamed the claimant. There is no defence if the claimant can prove malice or negligence

Damages and reform

It used to be the case that defamation remained as one of the few civil actions that was tried by a jury. The proceedings can be lengthy and costly. Damages awarded by a jury amount to unrealistically large sums.

The Courts and Legal Services Act 1990 confers power to the court of appeal to review jury award and to order a retrial. In *John v Mirror Group* (1996), £350,000 damages was awarded by the jury to the singer Elton John. By virtue of the 1990 Act, the Court of Appeal reduced the award to £75,000. They went on to call upon the judges at first instance to address to juries that damages should be equated to those for personal injuries but not to 'contemptuous' damages which aims at punishing a defendant as well as compensating the plaintiff. Jury trial remains for some cases. The 1996 Act provides an alternative of summary procedure where a judge sitting alone can dispose of a case, declare the statements in the question to be false and defamatory and order for correction, apology, damages of up to £10,000 or injunction. With many matters being resolved at this summary stage, together with the ruling in *John v Mirror*, one can expect that future defamation awards will be significantly reduced and matters be disposed of more efficiently and with much less costs. More cases may come in front of the courts in due course.

6 Family Law

You should be familiar with the following areas:

- elements of a valid marriage
- formalities, in particular, the Church of England ceremony
- what are void and voidable marriages
- facts for divorce and the two decrees
- financial settlement mainly on maintenance claims before and after divorce

Elements of a valid marriage

Marriage has been defined as 'the voluntary union for life of one man and one woman to the exclusion of all others' (*Hyde v Hyde* (1866)). This is the concept of monogamy. In the UK, bigamy is a crime. It used to be the case that a person could be sued for breach of a promise of marriage (that is, engagement), but the Law Reform (Miscellaneous Provisions) Act 1970 has changed this. Cohabitation is not legally recognised as being the same as marriage, at least not yet in this country; therefore, many rights and duties arising from a marriage will not be applicable to couples who only live together.

A valid marriage must have the following elements:

Age

The Age of Marriage Act 1929 provides that both parties to a marriage must be 16 years of age or over otherwise the marriage is void. If either party is between 16 and 18 years old, consent must be given by both parents. If the parents are not alive or otherwise unavailable, a list of other persons from whom consent can be obtained can be found in Sched 2 of the Marriage Act 1949. If the required consent is refused, the parties may apply to the court (usually, the magistrates' court) which will make a decision after considering what is in the best interest of the minor. It should be noted that a marriage without the required consent will still be valid but the parties involved can be accused of some kind of fraud, either because they have lied about their ages or have forged consent papers at the time of marriage.

Relatives outside the prohibited degrees

The Marriage Act 1949, as amended by the Marriage (Prohibited Degrees of Relationships) Act 1986, provides a list of relatives within the prohibited degrees to whom a person cannot marry. This is a long and detailed list and the obvious ones are father to daughter, mother to son, brothers, sisters and a person to his or her parent-in-law unless his or her former spouse and the in-law's spouse are dead. The reasons for the prohibited degrees are partly based on moral grounds and partly because of the possibility of genetic risk for the offspring of the marriage.

Neither party is in an existing marriage

If a party in a marriage is already married, then the second marriage is void and the crime of bigamy may have been committed, contrary to s 57 of the Offences Against the Person Act 1861. The maximum punishment for bigamy is seven years' imprisonment. Normally, a person would want to make sure he is divorced before engaging in another marriage. Failing this, an accused may still have a defence against a bigamy charge if he or she believes in good faith and on reasonable grounds that the spouse is dead or that the first marriage has been dissolved or annulled. Further, the Matrimonial Causes Act 1973 allows a person to make an application to the court for decree of presumption of death and dissolution of marriage. The person must show that the spouse has been continuously absent for seven years and he has no cause to believe that the spouse is still alive. Alternatively, the person could obtain a divorce, relevant grounds being two years desertion and five years separation. Both require a shorter time scale to dissolve a marriage. It is often on emotional grounds that an applicant chooses this route rather than a divorce and sometimes on inheritance consideration since a divorcee is not entitled to inherit his or her spouse's or his or her spouse's relatives' estate.

The parties are of opposite sex

It is not possible under English law to legally register a homosexual marriage. A person's sex is determined biologically at their birth. In recent years, there have been a few cases where transsexuals wished to change their sexual entry on their birth certificates but failed. In *X, Y and Z v UK* (1997), the transsexual applicant wished to be registered as the father of his inseminated child in the UK and brought his case to the European Court of Human Rights but lost. The European Court pointed out that the law on granting parental rights to transsexuals, artificial insemination and the role of the father was in a transitional stage throughout Europe and, hence, it allowed the domestic law in the UK a wide margin of application. This also signalled that the law in these areas might change rapidly.

Formalities

A marriage ceremony and the procedure before it has to be carried out and solemnised as provided by the Marriage Acts 1949 and 1983. If there is a basic defect in the marriage procedure or ceremony, the marriage will be void. A marriage may be solemnised by a Church of England ceremony or superintendent registrar's certificate.

Church of England ceremony

There are four ways in which the church may conduct a ceremony:

- *Banns to be published announcing the forthcoming wedding on three Sundays in the church*

  During this time, anyone can raise any cause or just impediment to stop the marriage. If no such impediment or cause is raised, or is raised, but is not justified, then the wedding can take place on the proposed day.

- *Common licence to be issued by or on behalf of a bishop*

  If the parties swear that no impediment exists, and either has resided within the parish for at least three months, then they can marry in a church or chapel within that parish.

- *Superintendent registrar's certificate to be obtained allowing the wedding to be carried out in either party's local church*

  The residence requirement is only seven days, but before the certificate is issued, notice of marriage has to be publicised in the church for at least 21 clear days and the parties have to declare that no impediment exists.

- *Special licence issued by or on behalf of the Archbishop of Canterbury*

  This is rare (only about 500 each year) but, if granted, a wedding can take place immediately and anywhere.

111

A wedding under the Church of England must take place between 8 am and 6 pm and must be witnessed by at least two persons. It should now be understood that a couple cannot just walk into a church, bring two friends as witnesses and ask the clergyman to marry them. Such scenarios do appear in examination questions.

Superintendent registrar's certificate and licence

- *Certificate*

    Notice of marriage is given to the local superintendent registrar and the solemn declaration of no impediment is made. If the parties live in different areas each party has to give notice to his or her registrar. The public are able to inspect the notice and, after 21 clear days, a certificate can be issued and the couple may marry in any registrar's office in the country by appointment or in a registered building by a registrar or another authorised person (usually a religious minister). Again, the wedding must take place between 8 am and 6 pm and must have at least two witnesses. The doors must be open. Certificates which allow exceptions to these conditions can also be obtained to follow the customs of Society of Friends and of those of the Jewish Faith (that is, a wedding behind closed doors, without time restrictions and without witnesses).

- *Licence*

    This is a quicker procedure by which a couple can be married after having given one clear day notice of marriage to the superintendent registrar. Only one party of the intended marriage is required to give such notice. The residential requirement is that the person has lived within the local area of the registrar for at least 15 days and the other party is present in the country when the notice is given. Where the circumstances are extraordinary (for example, a death bed marriage) a Registrar General's licence can also be obtained to permit a wedding to be carried out somewhere other than a registered building or a registry office.

Void and voidable marriage

A void marriage is simply an invalid marriage which the law regards as non-existent. The parties are still single. There is no need to apply to a court to nullify such a marriage. However, for the sake of certainty, one can sometimes formally apply to an appropriate court for a decree of nullity. Section 11 of the Matrimonial Causes Act 1973 sets out the circumstances in which a marriage is void. These are:

- marriages within the prohibited degrees;
- either party was already married;
- the parties were not respectively male and female;
- either party had entered a polygamous marriage while being domiciled in England and Wales.
- either party is under 16 years old;
- there is a basic defect in the marriage ceremony.

A voidable marriage is legally valid, but because of certain circumstances, an appropriate court can annul it on the petition of one or both parties. The grounds for such an application are set out in s 12 of the Matrimonial Causes Act 1973:

- the marriage had not been consummated owing to the incapacity or the wilful refusal to consummate it;
- either party did not validly consent to the marriage, whether in consequence of duress, mistake, unsoundness of mind (for example, because of an illness, drink or drugs) or otherwise;
- either party was suffering from mental disorder within the meaning of the Mental Health Act 1983 at the time of the marriage rendering the person unfit to marry;
- the respondent was suffering from venereal disease in a communicable form at the time of the marriage and the applicant did not know it;
- the respondent was pregnant by some person other than the petitioner at the time of the marriage and the applicant did not know it.

For the last four grounds, the petition must be taken out within three years from the date of the marriage.

Divorce

Divorce brings marriage to an end. The rights and duties of a husband and wife also end there. In the event of intestacy, a divorcee will no longer be entitled to inherit any part of his or her ex-spouse's estate.

Where there is a will, a divorce will automatically revoke any gift to a former spouse and the appointment of the ex-spouse as an executor or executrix. The party is then free to remarry. The person who initiates the divorce proceedings is called the petitioner and the other party is the respondent.

The Matrimonial and Family Proceedings Act 1987 requires that no divorce petition can be presented until one year has expired from the date of the marriage. Section 1(1) of the Matrimonial Causes Act (MCA) 1973 sets out the only one ground for divorce, that is, that the marriage has irretrievably broken down. This ground can be proven by one of the five facts set out in s 1(2)(a)–(e) of the MCA. In other words, a petitioner can only rely on one of the five facts stated in the Act for a divorce and a judge will not grant a divorce if he is not satisfied that one of the facts has been shown. These are:

Adultery

The respondent has committed adultery and the petitioner finds it intolerable to live with the respondent. Adultery is the voluntary sexual intercourse between two persons, one or both of whom are married but not to each other.

Unreasonable behaviour

The respondent has behaved in such a way that the petitioner cannot reasonably be expected to live with the respondent. Examples of unreasonable behaviour include violence, extreme bad temper, drunkenness, obsessive jealousy and many others.

Desertion

The respondent has deserted the petitioner without his or her consent for a continuous period of at least two years immediately proceeding the presentation of the petition. As long as the petitioner can prove this, there is no need for the respondent to give consent to the divorce. If the petitioner had agreed to the 'desertion' arrangement, it was no longer a desertion but a separation. The petitioner will then have to obtain consent to the divorce from the other party if they wish to rely on the fact of two years separation; otherwise the petitioner will have to wait until the separation has lasted for five years (see below).

Separation for two years

The parties have lived apart continuously for at least two years immediately before the presentation of the petition and the respondent has consented that the divorce decree be granted.

Separation for five years

If a respondent does not give his or her consent for a divorce, a petitioner can still have a divorce if he or she can show that the parties have lived apart for at least five years.

For the meaning of separation and desertion, living together under one roof, but following completely separate lives, counts. It is strong evidence if the parties do not even have their meals together at all.

Some procedural aspects and the two decrees

Divorce is normally commenced by filing a petition and relevant documents in a county court. Over 90% of petitions are uncontested and these are sometimes called 'postal divorce' because the parties are generally not required to attend any court hearing. Once the judge is satisfied that the ground has been established and no issues to do with children are involved, a *decree nisi* will be announced in an open court. The parties are informed when this takes place but they are not required to attend. The *decree nisi* recognises that the marriage has irretrievably broken down and announces that the marriage be dissolved unless sufficient cause be shown to the Court within six weeks as to why the final decree should not be made. After these six weeks, the petitioner is entitled to apply for what is called a decree absolute. There are, however, circumstances where the petitioner is in no hurry to apply for the decree absolute. There may be financial matters which are not yet resolved or the petitioner may not want to make it convenient for the respondent who has been involved with a third party. If this is the case, the respondent may apply after a further three months have expired. Regarding the topic of *decree nisi* and decree absolute, there are two areas of frequent confusion and it should be made clear here:

- the six week time gap between the two decrees is not a cooling down period;
- the *decree nisi* has not yet terminated the marriage. If either party suddenly dies after the *decree nisi* is granted, but before a decree absolute, the inheritance rules will take effect as if the parties were still husband and wife. The legal relationship will not end until a decree absolute is granted.

Judicial separation

This is when the parties want a separation which is recognised by law but not a divorce. The reasons for this are usually religious or relating to children. The petitioner has to rely on one of the same five facts for divorce but does not need to show that the marriage has irretrievably broken down. The one year rule does not apply. There is only one decree and the effect of it is to release the parties from the duty to cohabit.

Apart from petitioning for a judicial separation, the parties can sometimes agree a separation agreement which may also deal with the issues of property ownership, access and custody of children of the family and some provision for maintenance. One main purpose of a separation agreement is to provide evidence for a later divorce. Regarding maintenance and property ownership, the court may vary what the parties have agreed if the issue is put in front of it in a later day.

Financial settlement and some issues relating to the children of the family

When a marriage breaks down, there are many matters which need resolving. The obvious ones are the financial aspects before and after the divorce and the arrangement regarding the children.

Regarding financial settlement, the parties can come to an agreement and then provide required personal details to the court and ask the court to make a so called consent order. The court tends not to intervene but this is not a rubber stamping exercise. If the court sees that there are extraordinary or unfair situations, or that it is not within its power to make certain terms agreed, it will not make the order.

Both parties by consent, or either party alone, can make an application to the court for one or more of the orders stated below and ss 22–24 of the MCA list out the types of orders that the court has the power to make:

- *Periodical payments pending suit*

  Available before decree absolute for both the spouse and the children of the family. Application for this type of order can be made anytime during the divorce proceedings and is often made at the commencement.

- *Periodical payments after the divorce, a lump sum payment and a property adjustment order to a spouse*

  Application for these can be made anytime during the divorce proceedings but it will not be heard until a *decree nisi* has been granted and the order will not take effect until the decree is made absolute. Periodical payments can be secured on a property (that is, like a mortgage against a house). The court can also order a lump sum payment to be paid by instalments. Examples of property adjustment orders include orders for an outright transfer of the ownership of a property from a party to another and for varying the existing ownership proportion between the parties.

- *Periodical payments and lump sum payments to a child*

  Available to a child of the family or to a person (including the spouse) for the benefit of a child of the family. The court can accept application and make an order for this type of order anytime during the divorce proceedings. The order can take effect immediately and for periodical payments even be backdated to the date of the application.

- *Property adjustment order to a child*

  Available to a child of the family or a person for the benefit of a child of the family can be made but this is very rare.

- *Order for sale*

  The court has the power to order a property to be sold in appropriate circumstances.

Section 25A of the MCA imposes a duty on the court to consider early termination of dependence without undue hardship to a party whenever it is appropriate. For example, a wife is attending college and she will complete her course in two years. The court may order a larger lump sum to be paid to her but restrict the duration of the periodical payments for three years when she would be expected to become financially independent. This type of order is often described as a 'clean break order'. Under the Pensions Act 1995, the court now has powers to make orders which directly deals with pensions of the parties on marriage breakdown.

On an application, the court can vary orders of maintenance pending suit, periodical payments, secured periodical payments, instalments of a lump sum but not the lump sum itself and orders for sale of a property. This is particularly relevant if the financial circumstances of the parties have changed. The court has no power to vary a lump sum order or a property adjustment order.

Factors in making financial settlement orders

Section 25(1) of the MCA provides that it is the duty of the court, when making a financial settlement order, to look into all the circumstances of the case, first consideration being given to the welfare of any children of the family under 18 years of age.

Section 25(2) sets out a non-exhaustive list of factors for the court to consider when making an order for a spouse. These are:

(a) the income, earning capacity, property and other financial resources of the parties;

(b) the financial needs, obligations and responsibilities of the parties;

(c) the standard of living enjoyed before the breakdown of the marriage;

(d) the age of the parties and the duration of the marriage;

(e) any physical or mental disabilities of the parties;

(f) contributions made to the welfare of the family in the past and the foreseeable future. This includes any contribution by looking after the home or caring for the family;

(g) the conduct of the parties.

Section 25(3) of the MCA provides guidelines relevant to the making of an order for a child. The courts' attention has been drawn to the manner in which the child has been brought up and how the parties expected him to be educated and trained. Apart from this, these guidelines are not too different from those stated in s 25(2) above. Of course, s 25(2)(d), (f) and (g) are not likely to be relevant for a child and the personal factors refer to the child rather than to the parties (that is, the income and physical disability of the child instead of the parties, etc).

One last point to mention is that, since the Child Support Act 1991, the court orders on maintenance payments for children of families whose financial resources are within the Child Support Agencies' financial ceiling have been superseded by the Agencies' assessments. Applications to the court for financial orders for children are still applicable to wealthier families.

Regarding children of the family, the parties can make arrangements privately but if failed or for the sake of certainty either party can apply to the court for a so called 'section 8 order' under the Children Act 1989. Section 8 orders include a residence order (previously a custody order), a contact order (for visits, access, stay, etc), a specific issue order (for example, education, medical treatment, surname to be changed and taking the child out of the country) and a prohibited step order (for example, to prevent a child from receiving a certain type of medical treatment and being taken out of the jurisdiction).

7 Law of Succession

You should be familiar with the following areas:

- **rules of intestacy**
- **requirements of a valid will**
- **soldiers' will**
- **revocation of a will**
- **provisions for family and dependants**

Introduction and various types of property

The law of succession is concerned with the transfer of properties of a dead person to new owners. There are two main categories of property, that is, real property and personal property (also called personalty). Real property describes only freehold land and a gift of real property in a will is called a 'devise'. Freehold land is supposed to be inherited through the generations of the owner forever. A gift of personal property under a will is called a 'legacy' or a 'bequest'. There are three main types of personalty:

(a) *Leasehold property in land*

Such a lease can be for a term of a few months or a few years and it can be for a long lease of say 99 or even 999 years. The land will revert back to the freeholder when the term of the lease expires. Many long leases for residential properties only require payments of a symbolic rent (sometimes, only a peppercorn). The Leasehold Reform Act 1967 provides that such a tenant, who has occupied the house or part of it as his only or main residence for the last three years or three out of the last 10 years, is entitled to buy the freehold or obtain a 50 year extension of his lease at a statutory rate if the parties fail to agree a price. For properties in the provinces, we are talking about a few hundred pounds rather than thousands here. In London, this sum can be quite significant.

(b) *Moveable things (sometimes called chattels or tangibles)*

These include almost everything around us except for land which is not moveable and other legal rights such as debt which is intangible. Your books, pens, desk, hi-fi, computer, CDs, watches, clothing and many other things are all your personal moveable property.

(c) *Intangibles*

These are things that one cannot physically touch and are mostly legal rights such as debts, shares, copyrights, patents, computer programs, and so on.

The duty of transferring property from the deceased to a new owner falls on the personal representatives of the deceased. When there is a valid will at the time of death, the personal representatives are called executors and, if there is intestacy (that is, death without leaving a will or a valid will), the personal representatives are called 'administrators'. The basic duties of the personal representatives are to collect all money and property, pay all debts, then distribute the estate to its rightful owners.

Intestacy

This describes the situation when a person dies without leaving a valid will at the time of death. The Administration of Estates Act 1925 provides detailed rules governing whom is entitled to the estate. There are four primary situations:

(a) *If the intestate leaves issue, the spouse takes:*

- all the personal chattels absolutely; and
- £125,000 plus interest from the death to the payment; then
- the balance to be divided into two halves.

The issue take one half and the spouse has a life interest of the other half. The issue will also take this latter half when the spouse dies.

Issue are a person's children, grandchildren and subsequent direct descendants. For the purpose of succession, adopted children and illegitimate children are included. A spouse's children not born to the person, if not adopted yet, are excluded. The owner of a life interest can only take the income generated from but not the property itself. If the property is a lump sum of money, the owner of the life interest can take the interest every month or year generated from the money but is not entitled to touch the capital. If the property is a house, he is entitled to receive the rent but cannot sell the house. If it is an apple tree, he can keep the apples every year but has no right to chop the tree down. When the life interest holder dies, the property will go to the remainder holder who can do whatever he wants with it.

(b) *If the intestate leaves no issue but a parent or brother or sister of the whole blood or their issue, the spouse takes:*

- all the personal chattels absolutely;
- £200,000 plus interest from the death to the payment; and
- half of the balance of the estate absolutely (see (d), below, for the treatment of the other half).

(c) *If the intestate leaves neither issue nor parents, brothers nor sisters of the whole blood or their issue, the spouse takes the whole estate absolutely.*

(d) After the spouse has taken, as stated in points (a) and (b) above, or if the person has no spouse (that is, being single, spouse predeceased or divorced), the estate goes to:

- the issue but if none; to
- parents but if none; to
- brothers and sisters of the whole blood in equal shares (or issue of a deceased one).

If there is no surviving spouse nor any surviving relatives as above, then the estate goes to:

- brothers and sisters of the half blood in equal shares (or issues of a deceased one) but if none; to
- grandparents but if none; to
- uncles and aunts of the whole blood in equal shares (or issue of a deceased one) but if none; to
- uncles and aunts of the half blood in equal shares (or issue of a deceased one) but if none; to
- the Crown: this is the situation known as *bona vacantia*.

One last point which should be noted is that, if any of the entitled relatives are under 18 years of age, the property will be held in trust until they reach adulthood or are married earlier.

Making a will

A will is a declaration by a person concerning the distribution of property after death. A man making a will is called a 'testator' and a woman is called a 'testatrix'. The person must have the required capacity in general, meaning that he should be aged 18 or over, and of sound mind, being capable of understanding the nature of what he is doing (*Banks v Goodfellow* (1870)). The legal formalities are set out in the Wills Act 1837 and Administration of Justice Act 1982. No will shall be valid unless:

(a)   it is in writing and signed by the testator, or by some other person in his presence and by his direction and it is apparent that the testator intended that his signature would give effect to the will; and

(b)   the signature is made or acknowledged by the testator in the joint presence of two or more witnesses; and

(c)   each witness either attests and signs the will or acknowledges his signature in the presence of the testator.

Therefore, it should be noted that:

• A will must be in writing for obvious reasons. A signature cannot be made on an audio tape. It can be written on any type of paper or parchment and it can be handwritten, typed or printed. In the case of *Barnes* (1926), the will was written on an eggshell and was held to be valid.

• A signature can be a thumbprint, a seal, a stamp mark or simply a mark. As long as the testator intends it to be his signature giving effect to the will, it is sufficient. Section 17 of the Administration of Justice Act 1982 now provides that the signature of the testator can be made anywhere on the will (not necessarily at the end) but it should be made or acknowledged after the will has all been written (*Wood v Smith* (1992)).

• A witness must be able to see the signature of the testator and, therefore, a blind person could not be a competent witness. The person however does not have to see the action of the actual signing. The testator can sign the will earlier but he must acknowledge to the witness that the signature is his.

• When the testator signs or acknowledges his signature, at least two witnesses must be present at the same time (that is, joint presence).

When the witness attests the will, the other witness does not have to be there.

- The witnesses do not need to read or know the contents of the will. It used to be the case that any gift in a will to a witness would fail but, since the Wills Act 1968, a beneficial witness will receive his gift if there are two or more other witnesses to the will apart from him.

If the testator wishes to incorporate other documents in the will, the documents have to be:

(a) in existence at the time of execution of the will;

(b) referred in the will as already existing;

(c) clearly identified in or identifiable from the will.

Wills of soldiers, sailors and airmen

Section 7 of the Wills Act 1837, as extended by the Wills (Soldiers and Sailors) Act 1918, have granted special privileges to soldiers, sailors and airmen on actual military service and seamen at sea. Such persons may make wills without complying with the formalities as stated in the previous section. A will can be made without any witness and it can be made orally. There is, however, one restriction which is that the testator has to be aged 14 or over.

Obviously, if this type of will is made orally there must be a person who can tell others the wishes of the soldier. The late Lord Denning gave a very wide interpretation of what it meant by 'soldier on actual military service' in his *ratio* in the case of *Re Wingham* (1949). It is understood that it includes men and women serving or called up for service in war, those engaged in or about to proceed to hostilities and those involved in military operations overseas. It includes not only the fighting men but also those who serve in the forces such as doctors, nurses, chaplains and so forth. In the case, a trainee pilot on a RAF instruction course in Canada was held to be on actual military service. In *Re Jones* (1981), the privilege has been extended to a soldier serving in Northern Ireland. Jones was shot and on the way to hospital he said to two officers, 'If I do not make it, make sure Anne (his fiancée) gets all my stuff'. It was held that this statement was his last will even though he had made a formal will leaving his estate to his mother.

All informal wills remain valid even after hostilities or emergencies have ended.

Revocation

A will can be revoked in many ways, sometimes by the testators taking certain actions and sometimes by the operation of the law. If a will is to be revoked in writing, it has to be done in the same manner as the will was made, that is, it has to be signed in the joint presence of at least two witnesses who attest the document in the presence of the testator. A piece of paper signed by the testator and attested by two witnesses stating that his will is revoked is a valid revocation. The witnesses here do not have to be the witnesses who attested the original will. If it is only signed by the testator and not witnessed, his last will will not be revoked therefore will still take effect. A will can be wholly or partly revoked. Wills usually begin with a clause revoking all former wills. If this is not the case, the testator's last will will still take effect except for those parts which are inconsistent with the new will. Let us look at an example. In his last will, A leaves item X to B, item Y to C and the rest of his estate to D and, in his new will, (without revocation clause), A leaves item X to E and £500 to F. The effect is that item X will go to E, item Y will still go to C, F will receive £500 and D will get the rest less £500.

If a person wants to amend his will, he can either make a new will or he can execute a document called *codicil* to make amendments. This is particularly appropriate when he does not want to revoke his previous will but only wants to change or add a few gifts. A *codicil* is sometimes described as an insertion or attachment to a will and must be formalised in the same way as a will. A testator can also make amendments in the original will, say by crossing out some parts of it. Again, the least that he has to do is to sign the amendments and have two witnesses to attest his signature. This may not be very professional but will be legally effective.

Section 20 of the Wills Act 1837 also provides that a will can be revoked by the burning, tearing or otherwise destroying the same by the testator, or by some person in his presence and by his direction, with the intention of revoking the same. Destruction by accident will not suffice. If a will cannot be found or has been destroyed without being revoked, its contents may be proved by other evidence such as a draft, a copy or oral evidence (*Sugden v Lord St Leonards* (1876)). Destruction can be a partial one. The main issue here is whether the testator intended his act to take effect as a revocation of the will. Tearing off the signature and attestation clause has been held to be a valid revocation. In *Re Adams* (1990), the testatrix informed her solicitor of her intention and asked the will to be sent back to her. After her death, the will was found and it had been heavily scribbled and it was impossible to read the signatures. The court held that the will was revoked.

A will can also be revoked by the operation of law without the testator having taken any action. By s 18 of the Wills Act 1837, as amended by the Administration of Justice Act 1982 adding a sub-s 18A, a will is revoked by a subsequent marriage of a testator or testatrix. However, it will not be revoked if it appears from the will that at the time it was made the testator was expecting to be married to a particular person and that it was intended that the will should not be revoked by the marriage. The name of the spouse and the intention should therefore be stated clearly in the will to bring effect to this section. Section 18A further provides that a subsequent divorce or nullity of a marriage revokes any gift to the former spouse and the appointment of the spouse in the will as executor or trustee. Other parts of the will remain effective.

Provisions for family and dependants

The Inheritance (Provision for Family and Dependants) Act 1975 provides that a person who is not provided for reasonably from a will, an intestacy or from both may apply to the courts to obtain such provision out of the estate. Who can apply then?

Section 1(1) of the 1975 Act provides a list:

(a) the wife or husband of the deceased;

(b) a former wife or former husband of the deceased who has not remarried;

(c) a child of the deceased;

(d) any person (not being a child of the deceased) who, in the case of any marriage to which the deceased was at any time a party, was treated by the deceased as a child of the family in relation to that marriage;

(e) any person (not being a person included in the foregoing paragraphs of this subsection) who immediately before the death of the deceased was being maintained, either wholly of partly, by the deceased.

It should be noted that there is no age or marriage limit here. In *Re: Callaghan* (1984), a man over 40 years old who was treated as a child of the family since he was 12 made a successful claim under the Act. Sub-section (d) covers a spouse's child from a previous marriage. Sub-section (e) covers anybody who can satisfy the condition of maintenance. If a person gave £200 every month to his old aunt before his death, then the old lady can make a claim if nothing is left to her in his will or if he had not left a will and his brothers and sisters have inherited his estate. Another example can be that a deceased lived with his girlfriend and gave her £600 per month. In his will, he had only left her his car. The fact was when he made the will, he did not know her so well and they did not live together. There was £30,000 worth of properties and money not disposed of by his will (that is, a part intestacy situation) but, according to the intestacy rule, this part of the estate would not go to his girlfriend. This has then become a situation where the girlfriend has not been reasonably provided for from both his will and his intestacy and the lady is entitled to apply under the 1975 Act.

The next question is what the Act means by reasonable financial provision. There are two standards, one applicable to a spouse and the other to other applicants. To a spouse, it is whatever is reasonable in all circumstances, whether or not it is needed for maintenance. For others, it is whatever is reasonable in all circumstances actually needed for their maintenance. One can therefore expect a spouse to be entitled to more than others would. Application has to be made within six months of the grant of probate or letters of administration. In deciding a case, the court will take into consideration all the relevant circumstances including any statements made by the deceased as to the reasons why certain provisions were or were not made. Examples of relevant statements include 'I have not left anything to Peter in my will because I gave him £20,000 last Christmas, and I do not want to leave anything to Mary because she never came to see me for over six months since we had an argument'.

8 Freedom under the Law

You should be familiar with the following areas:

- the concept of individual rights under the Human Rights Act 1998 as opposed to the traditional civil liberties
- freedoms of movement, speech, association, assembly and procession and their limitations
- freedom from race and sex discrimination
- the means of protection of individual freedoms and rights

Introduction

We often say 'this is a free country'. Indeed, we do possess certain civil freedoms and liberties, such as freedom of speech, freedom of movement and freedom of association, assembly and procession. The UK does not have a written constitution; therefore, these are freedoms and liberties assumed for citizens by virtue of being subjects of the Queen rather than rights which are conferred by law. A society cannot be totally 'free'; this would bring chaos and a state of anarchy. Some behaviour, which may harm others or the society as a whole, is prohibited. As a result, freedoms have to be restricted. With this background, when the topic of freedom under the law is discussed lawyers often refer to the laws that limit and restrict the assumed freedoms rather than any rights which are provided by law.

In recent years, a fundamental change has occurred since the enactment of the Human Rights Act 1998. The purpose of the Act is to incorporate into UK law the rights provided for in the Articles and Protocols of the European Convention of Human Rights and Fundamental Freedoms 1950. These rights and fundamental freedoms called the 'Convention rights' in the Act, include:

Article 2 on right to life.

Article 3 on prohibition of torture.

Article 4 on prohibition of slavery and forced labour.

Article 5 on right to liberty and security.

Article 6 on right to a fair trial.

Article 7 on no punishment without law.

Article 8 on right to privacy and family life.

Article 9 on freedom of thought, conscience and religion.

Article 10 on freedom of expression.

Article 11 on freedom of assembly and association.

Article 12 on the right to marry.

Article 13 on prohibition of discrimination.

Article 1 of the First Protocol on protection of property.

Article 2 of the First Protocol on right to education.

Article 3 of the First Protocol on right to free elections.

Article 1 of the Sixth Protocol on abolition of the death penalty.

Article 2 of the Sixth Protocol regarding death penalty in times of war.

Only a small proportion of the Act is currently in force and the whole will be fully implemented on 2 October 2000. The UK was a member of the treaty for over 50 years but no law has been enacted to adopt the Convention until recently. In the past, judges were only influenced by the terms of the Convention which might find ways to emerge from the common law. The general view was that the Convention did not bind our courts and, if a person disagreed with a decision on a human right issue, he had to bring his case to the European Court of Human Rights in Strasbourg. The position is changing now. The 1998 Act confers the Convention rights to individuals and the Convention has become a formal source of legal rights and duties in the country. Bringing human rights cases to the European Court of Human Rights has been an extremely expensive and long process. By virtue of the Human Rights Act, individuals can bring a case regarding the Convention rights in our domestic courts cheaper and quicker. Section 2 provides that a court or tribunal, when determining a question which has arisen in connection with a Convention right, must take into account any judgment, decision, declaration or advisory opinion of the European Court of Human Rights and any opinions or decisions of the Convention Commissions and the Committee of Ministers. Section 3 provides that primary and subordinate legislation must be read and given effect in a way which is compatible with the Convention rights. Section 19 is already in force. It provides that a Minister in charge of a Bill in either House of Parliament must, before Second Reading, make a statement to the effect either that, in his view, the provisions of the Bill are compatible with the Convention rights or that, although he is unable to make a statement of compatibility, the government nevertheless wishes the House to proceed with the Bill. When the entire Act comes into force, judges will have the power to make formal declarations where UK laws conflict with the Convention rights. This is not to empower the Courts to strike down offending Acts but to enable judges to prompt Parliament to change the law. The Act further provides a fast track process to amend the law swiftly. In this way, the terms of the Convention will be upheld and the Parliamentary Supremacy is said to have been preserved. It can be foreseen that the Act will have significant impact in many areas of our law and will create a considerable change to our legal landscape.

Regarding individual freedoms, we shall now look into freedom of speech, freedom of movement, freedom of association, assembly and procession.

Freedom of speech/expression

Article 10 of the Convention regarding freedom of expression provides that:

1 Everyone has the right to freedom of expression. This right shall include freedom to hold opinions and to receive and impart information and ideas without interference by public authority and regardless of frontiers. This Article shall not prevent States from requiring the licensing of broadcasting, television or cinema enterprises.

2 The exercise of these freedoms, since it carries with it duties and responsibilities, may be subject to such formalities, conditions, restrictions or penalties as are prescribed by law and are necessary in a democratic society, in the interests of national security, territorial integrity or public safety, for the prevention of disorder or crime, for the protection of health or morals, for the protection of the reputation or rights of others, for preventing the disclosure of information received in confidence, or for maintaining the authority and impartiality of the judiciary.

Currently, freedom of speech (not 'right' yet) is assumed in our society but is restricted by:

(a) The law of defamation in tort.

(b) The Obscene Publications Acts 1959 and 1964, which aim at outlawing pornography on one hand and protecting genuine literature and art on the other. The Acts make it an offence to publish an obscene article whether for gain or not or to have an obscene article in one's possession, ownership or control for the purpose of publication for gain. Obscene articles, in short, are articles which 'tend to deprave and corrupt persons'. They are not confined to sexual material. Other matters which have been inserted include material concerning drug taking and violence. The 'Article' described in the Act may be a book, pictures, film, record, video cassette and so forth.

(c) The Children and Young Persons (Harmful Publications) Act 1955, which outlaws horror comics which illustrate crimes, violence, cruelty, incidents of a repulsive or horrible nature, which tend to corrupt the young.

(d) Censorship and classification of motion pictures by the British Board of Film Classification. The Theatres Act 1968 abolished the censorship of plays but an obscene play can still be a subject of prosecution.

(e) The law regarding contempt of court. A person who published material which may be prejudicial to a fair criminal trial or civil proceedings or otherwise interfere with the course of justice can be held for contempt of court and the person is subject to punishment including being put into jail.

(f) The Official Secrets Acts 1911–39 and 1989, which prohibit the disclosure of material which may undermine national security.

(g) The Race Relations Act 1976 and the Sex Discrimination Act 1975, which seek to outlaw discrimination on the grounds of race and sex. Part III of the Public Order Act 1986 creates a variety of offences against stirring up racial hatred.

(h) Some indirect privacy laws such as the law of defamation, breach of confidence and trust. When the Human Rights Act 1998 comes into force, Art 8 will confer rights of privacy and family life to individuals.

Freedom of movement (civil liberty)

Article 5 of the Convention is concerned with individuals' right to liberty and security. It says:

1 Everyone has the right to liberty and security of person. No one shall be deprived of his liberty save in the following cases and in accordance with a procedure prescribed by law:

(a) the lawful detention of a person after conviction by a competent court;

(b) the lawful arrest or detention of a person for non-compliance with the lawful order of a court or in order to secure the fulfillment of any obligation prescribed by law;

(c) the lawful arrest or detention of a person effected for the purpose of bringing him before the competent legal authority on reasonable suspicion of having committed an offence or when it is reasonably considered necessary to prevent his committing an offence or fleeing after having done so;

(d) the detention of a minor by lawful order for the purpose of educational supervision or his lawful detention for the purpose of bringing him before the competent legal authority;

(e) the lawful detention of persons for the prevention of the spreading of infectious diseases, of persons of unsound mind, alcoholics or drug addicts or vagrants;

(f) the lawful arrest or detention of a person to prevent his effecting an unauthorised entry into the country or of a person against whom action is being taken with a view to deportation or extradition.

2 Everyone who is arrested shall be informed promptly, in a language which he understands, of the reasons for his arrest and of any charge against him.

3 Everyone arrested or detained in accordance with the provisions of para 1(c) of this Article shall be brought promptly before a judge or other officer authorised by law to exercise judicial power and shall be entitled to trial within a reasonable time or to release pending trial. Release may be conditioned by guarantees to appear for trial.

4 Everyone who is deprived of his liberty by arrest or detention shall be entitled to take proceedings by which the lawfulness of his detention shall be decided speedily by a court and his release ordered if the detention is not lawful.

5 Everyone who has been the victim of arrest or detention in contravention of the provisions of this Article shall have an enforceable right to compensation.

It appears that the current practice in Britain is generally compatible with Art 5. A person being wrongfully detained can issue a writ of habeas corpus for a speedy release. Further, there are civil actions available against false imprisonment, wrongful arrest and malicious prosecution.

Freedom of association, assembly and procession

Article 11 of the Convention is concerned with the freedom of assembly and association. It says:

1 Everyone has the right to freedom of peaceful assembly and to freedom of association with others, including the right to form and to join trade unions for the protection of his interests.

2 No restrictions shall be placed on the exercise of these rights other than such as are prescribed by law and are necessary in a democratic society in the interests of national security or public safety, for the prevention of disorder or crime, for the protection of health or morals or for the protection of the rights and freedoms of others. This Article shall not prevent the imposition of lawful restrictions on the exercise of these rights by members of the armed forces, of the police or of the administration of the State.

Some restrictions against freedom of assembly and association in this country include:

(a) Section 137 (1) of the Highway Act 1980 makes it an offence for a person wilfully obstructing the free passage along a highway and, therefore, assembly or procession on a highway without prior permission from an appropriate authority will likely be in breach of the Act. It could also be the tort of public nuisance. If the meeting is held without permission on a private person's land, it is a trespass.

(b) Section 70 of the Criminal Justice and Public Order Act 1994 inserts two sections, 14A and 14B, to the Public Order Act 1986 creating new offences against 'trespassory assemblies' which may result in serious disruption to the life of the community or in significant damage to land of 'historical, architectural, archaeological or scientific importance'. These new sections help to resolve problems such as the gatherings at the Stonehenge a few years ago.

(c) Parks and open spaces usually belong to the Crown or to a local authority. There are often regulations which control assemblies in these areas. Prior written permissions are often required before public gatherings are allowed.

(d) It is unlawful for 50 or more persons to meet within one mile of Westminster Hall when either or both Houses are sitting (the Seditious Meetings Act 1817). However, this restriction is only applicable against meetings 'for the purpose of alternation of matters in Church and State' and, therefore, school trips or tourists should have no problem to meet there!

(e)   Of course, when two or more persons meet to plan or perform an illegal act, it is the crime of conspiracy.

Regarding the control of processions, there are several relevant laws such as the offence of obstructing the highway as mentioned above. Part II of the Public Order Act 1986 attempts to provide a framework of law for the holding of processions and demonstrations and has created several offences and conditions:

(a) Public procession

The Act provides that seven days written notice must be given to hold a public procession, unless it is not practicable to give the advanced notice. If the police believe that the procession may result in serious public disorder or serious damage to property, they can give directions or impose conditions on the proposed procession. Such directions can include changing the route or prohibiting entry to certain public places. A chief officer of police may apply to the local council for a period of up to three months to ban any procession from being held in certain areas.

(b) Riot

Twelve or more persons present together who use or threaten unlawful violence for a common purpose and cause a person of reasonable firmness present at the scene to fear for his personal safety.

(c) Violent disorder

Three or more persons present together who use or threaten unlawful violence and their joint conduct would cause a person of reasonable firmness present at the scene to fear for his personal safety.

(d) Affray

One or more persons are guilty of affray if they use or threaten unlawful violence towards another and the conduct would cause a person of reasonable firmness present at the scene to fear for his safety.

(g) Provocation of violence and harrassment

There are other less serious offences created by the Act such as (a) provocation of violence by using threatening, abusive or insulting words or behaviour or; distributing or displaying to another person any writing, sign or other visible representation which is threatening, abusive or insulting; or (b) causing harassment, alarm or distress by the mentioned threatening, abusive or insulting means. When appropriate assault, battery and other similar crimes can be prosecuted as well.

It should also be noted that the offences under the Public Order Act 1986 do not only apply to processions and demonstrations. If two to three persons have a fight in a pub, a club or after a football match, they can be guilty of affray and if the disorder spreads they can be charged for violent disorder and beyond.

Freedom from race and sex discrimination

There is a rule of law that all men and women are equal. It is also one of the fundamental rights as set out in Art 14 of the Convention that a person should be free from discrimination on any grounds such as sex, race, colour, language, religion, political or other opinion, national or social origin, association with a national minority, property, birth or other status. In a positive sense we often pride ourselves for living in a multi-cultural society because it allows us to enjoy life more by having contacts with different cultures, including a variety of music, food, interests and thoughts. Openness also helps to promote our trades and businesses with other countries.

In Chapter 4, we have come across the Race Relations Act 1976 and the Sex Discrimination Act 1975 which outlaw racial and sex discrimination at work as well as in other aspects of life. Part III of the Public Order Act 1986 provides a range of offences against persons who use threatening, abusive or insulting words, behaviour or other means (for example, display, publishing or distributing written material; public performance of a play; distributing, showing or playing a recording and broadcasting) to stir up racial hatred or by which racial hatred is likely stirred up. Section 23 of the 1986 Act further provides an offence of being in possession of racially inflammatory material.

With the help of these laws and public education, it is hoped that one day our society will truly be free from any form of discrimination and provide equal opportunities for all.

Protection of freedoms and rights

It used to be the case that the terms in the European Convention of Human Rights was nothing more than influential to our judges' decisions. If a claimant disagreed with the court's decision on a human right issue, he would have to bring his case to Strasbourg. By the implementation of the Human Rights Act 1998 on 2 October 2000, the Convention rights will formally become our domestic law and our courts and other public authorities have the duties to uphold those human and fundamental rights. There is already a requirement for the appropriate minister to make a statement regarding the compatibility of a Bill to the Convention rights when introducing a Bill to Parliament. The Parliamentary Commissioner Act 1967 created the Parliamentary Commissioner for Administration and, hence, the national and local ombudsmen who receive and hear complaints of maladministration of government departments and their agencies, local and other public authorities. It is foreseen that more cases in relation to citizens' fundamental rights will be brought to our domestic courts by virtue of the Human Rights Act. The courts can help by the following means:

- declaring a piece of legislation to be incompatible to the Convention rights;
- interpreting and upholding the Convention rights;
- allowing a writ of habeas corpus against an unlawful detention;
- ordering a public authority to carry out its duty;
- declaring an action, a policy or a regulation of a public body to be *ultra vires*.

Rule of Law and the rules of natural justice

When a court decides cases and a public authority exercises powers conferred to them, they should enforce and give effect to the Rule of Law and the rules of natural justice.

The Rule of Law was first explained in the writings of AV Dicey (one of the greatest constitutional lawyers in the UK) in 1885. They include:

- No man shall be punished unless he has been convicted in an ordinary court of law for a breach of the law. This also leads to the presumption of innocence before a person is convicted.

- All men and women are equal before the law. This further implies that no one is above the law no matter how high a position or how worthy a person. Every citizen shall be subject to the same law.

- The rights of the individual are secured not by guarantees set down in a formal document (for example, a constitution) but by the judicial decisions made in the ordinary courts. Every subject has a right to appear before the courts to safeguard his freedoms and liberties. This constitutional position is now subject to modification after the Human Rights Act 1998.

The rules of natural justice are essentially unwritten rules of the common law. They are often used in legislation particularly when statutory procedures are drawn for when and where to file a complaint, where and who to hear the case and how to file an appeal where an individual disagrees with an official decision. There are two main concepts:

- *The rule against bias*

  This means that a person should not be involved in making a judicial decision in which he has an interest, however small such interest is. In *Dimes v Grand Junction Canal Co* (1852), the Lord Chancellor awarded the decision in favour of the company and the House of Lords set aside the judgment because it was found that he was a shareholder in the company. This is not to say that the Lord Chancellor had been biased nor indeed made the wrong decision but to uphold the rule against bias and the principle of 'justice should not only be done, but be seen to be done'. On this basis, MPs now have to declare their interests before sitting. A director of a company should not vote if the company is deciding on a contract in which the director has an interest.

- *The right to be heard*

  This is the principle which ensures that each party to any proceedings should have the opportunity of knowing the case against him and of stating his own case. It is not only the courts; many organisations practise this principle for examples in their disciplinary and grievance procedures.

9 Legal Process and Institutions

You should be familiar with the following areas:

- powers of arrest and an outline of the procedure on complaints against the police
- pre-trial procedures in the magistrates' court
- rules and conditions of bail
- procedures of trials in the magistrates' courts and the Crown Court
- sentencing in the magistrates' courts and the Crown Court
- pre-trial and trial procedures of civil claims
- criminal and civil legal aid and other legal advice available to laymen
- outline of the hierarchy of courts
- various courts and their composition
- the youth court and other functions of the magistrates' courts
- the types and purposes of tribunals
- the appointments and functions of juries and magistrates
- the work and training of barristers and solicitors and their immunity from negligence claims

Introduction

After we have studied where our law comes from and various aspects of law in practice, this chapter explains how and by whom laws are administered, gives an introduction to criminal and civil litigation and discusses where we can obtain legal advice. It is not only hoped that students will achieve good results in examinations but also amass the confidence to deal with legal issues by being familiar with the law and legal procedure.

Criminal procedure

Police power, court procedure and bail

Police power

The police play an important role in enforcing criminal law in our society. The law has conferred a variety of powers to the police for this purpose. These powers include the power of arrest, stop and search, entry and searching of premises, seizure and detention of suspects. The area of law is mostly consolidated in the Police and Criminal Evidence Act (PACE) 1984. The Act also imposes conditions and restrictions on the police when exercising the powers conferred in them. For the purpose of this book, we shall discuss the power of arrest in more detail and the conditions of police detention briefly .

Power of arrest

Arrest without a warrant

PACE 1984 confers power to a constable to arrest a person when he has reasonable grounds to suspect that the person has committed, is committing or is about to commit an arrestable offence. What then is an arrestable offence? Section 24 of PACE 1984 defines an arrestable offence to be:

- an offence for which the sentence is fixed by law (for example, life imprisonment for murder);
- an offence for which a first offender over 21 (not previously convicted) may be sentenced to five years' imprisonment or more.
- s 24 further sets out certain offences under the Customs and Excise Management Act 1979, the Official Secrets Act 1911 and 1920, the Sexual Offences Act 1956, the Theft Act 1968 and other corruption in office offences, together with attempting, conspiring, inciting, aiding, abetting, counselling or procuring of those offences to be arrestable offences, some of these offences do not carry prison sentences of five years or longer. Further, in legislation after PACE 1984, some offences are declared arrestable offences by the Acts which create them, for example, the Protection from Harassment Act 1997.

It is not only a constable who can arrest another person, the Act states that any person may arrest anyone who is committing or has committed an arrestable offence or whom the person has reasonable grounds for suspecting to be committing or have committed an arrestable offence. This is commonly known as a citizen's arrest; the main difference between this and a constable's arrest is that a private citizen cannot make an arrest if he suspects another is about to commit an arrestable offence – he has to wait until the offence is actually being committed. After a citizen's arrest, the relevant authority, most obviously the police, should be informed as soon as is practicably possible otherwise the person arrested may be able to sue for false imprisonment.

Other offences should be described as ' an offence which is not an arrestable offence'. There is no such thing as a non-arrestable offence because for an offence which is not an arrestable offence, a constable can still make an arrest as long as certain conditions are met. Section 25(1) goes on to say that, where a constable has reasonable grounds for suspecting that any offence which is not an arrestable offence has been committed or attempted, or is being committed or attempted, he may arrest the person if it appears to him that service of a summons is impracticable or inappropriate, for which sub-s (3) provides a few situations:

- unascertainable name or address of the person concerned;
- when an arrest is necessary to prevent the person from causing physical injury or damage to himself, others or property;
- when an arrest is necessary to prevent the person from committing an offence against public decency or an unlawful obstruction of the highway; and
- when an arrest is necessary to protect a child or other vulnerable person from harm.

Section 28 sets out that the person arrested must be informed of the reason for the arrest at the time of or as soon as practicable after the arrest. The person is usually cautioned by the statement 'You do not have to say anything but it may harm your defence if you do not mention when questioned something you may later rely on in court. Anything you do say may be given in evidence'. The police caution used to be 'You do not have to say anything unless you wish to do so but what you say may be given in evidence'. One will note that the right of silence has largely been curtailed.

Section 32 confers power to a constable to search a person after his arrest if the person is believed to present a danger to the police officer or others. A constable can also search the person for concealed evidence relating to the offence for which the person is arrested. If the search is conducted in public, the constable shall not require the person to remove any of his clothing other than an outer coat, jacket or gloves.

Arrest by warrant

After the police have investigated a particular crime, if they consider that there is enough evidence to charge a person, they normally make an application to the magistrates for a warrant. In an emergency, a magistrate may be visited at his home in the middle of the night. The police must furnish written information on oath for the magistrate to consider. If the warrant is issued, the magistrate may also direct that the arrested person be granted bail. The Criminal Justice Act 1967 provides that a warrant of arrest may not be issued against a person aged 17 or over unless the offence is indictable, punishable by imprisonment or the address of the defendant is not sufficiently established for the service of a summons on him.

Detention and police bail

After an arrest, if the police are satisfied that they have sufficient evidence, they should file a charge against the person. If charged, the person must be released on police bail unless, in general:

- the name and address of the person cannot be ascertained;
- it is for the person's own protection or preventing further injury or damage to property; or
- there are reasonable grounds to believe that the person may abscond or interfere with witness or justice.

If the person is kept in custody, he must be brought to the magistrates' court as soon as possible. If the police do not have sufficient evidence to charge, the normal maximum duration to detain a person without charge is 24 hours. A superintendent or higher rank officer may authorise continued detention for questioning for up to 36 hours where the offence in question is a serious arrestable offence. Serious arrestable offences are listed in s 116 and Sched 5 of PACE 1984 to include treason, murder, manslaughter, rape, kidnapping, some gross indecency and sexual offences, some firearms and explosives related offences, causing death by dangerous driving and many more. For such offences, further detention to 72 hours has to be authorised by a magistrate, then a further 24 hours if another warrant is issued by a magistrate. When these 96 hours have expired, the suspect has to be charged or released. Sections 56 and 58 of PACE 1984 confers to a person detained rights to have someone informed and to have access to legal advice but, again, if the offence is a serious arrestable offence, the police may withhold these rights for the first 36 hours of detention.

Complaints against the police

It is convenient in this section to discuss the procedure of making a complaint against the police. The Police Complaints Authority was established by PACE 1984. The idea of such an establishment was to set up an authority independent to the force. Their purpose is to see that, whenever a complaint is made about a police officer's conduct by a member of the public, the matter is dealt with thoroughly and fairly. Members of the authority are full time and come from many varied backgrounds. They should never have served as police officers.

A complaint should normally be brought within 12 months of the alleged incident. It can be initiated:

(a)   in writing directly to the Authority at 10 Great George Street, London;

(b)   in writing to the chief officer of the force concerned;

(c)   by reporting to a police station where a senior officer on duty will take details from the complainant.

Examples of complaints can be unlawful arrest, excessive force used by the police or simply a police officer being rude to the complainant. After a complaint is filed, the chief officer has the first duty to take steps to obtain or preserve relevant evidence. What happens next will depend on the seriousness of the complaint:

Less serious complaints

If the complainant consents and the chief officer (with the help of his subordinate officer) is satisfied that the complaint would not justify a criminal or disciplinary charge, an informal resolution may be arranged. A meeting may take place between the complainant and the accused officer and an explanation and an apology may be given.

Serious complaints

If the complainant does not give his consent, or if the complaint raises more serious allegations, the matter must be fully investigated by a senior police officer and then a report must be sent to the chief officer. For more serious complaints the chief officer may refer the case to the Police Complaints Authority as he sees fit. For the most serious complaints, where police officers have been accused of causing death or serious injury, the matter must be referred to the Authority before the investigation begins. The Authority will then supervise the investigation, which will include the approval of the appointment of the investigating officer, deciding on how the inquiry should be carried out and reading all the statements and seeing all the evidence. After the investigation, criminal charges or misconduct proceedings may be brought against the police officers. It may also be possible that the officers will only be given a formal warning or 'advice'. It should be noted that making a complaint does not affect the person's right to take the police to a civil court to sue for damages, though most claimants would choose to wait until the final outcome of the complaint.

Court procedure

The prosecution of a criminal case is often brought by the Crown on behalf of us all and, therefore, most criminal cases are called *R v Jones, Smith*, etc (that is, the surname of the defendant). 'R' stands for 'Regina' when a queen is on the throne and 'Rex' when we have a king. Some authorities (for example, the trading standards and the health and safety departments in a local council) are empowered to administer and prosecute certain legislation, then the council's name or even the surname of the person in charge may be used as the name of the prosecution in a criminal case. For some serious crimes, when the Director of Public Prosecutions is involved, their name will then appear as prosecution. The Crown Prosecution Service (CPS) was created by the Prosecution of Offences Act 1985. They are independent of the police and their duties do not only lie with prosecuting but also on deciding whether to prosecute a case. Of course, for very minor crimes, the police may directly provide information to the Court for the issue of a summons and if the defendant pleads guilty by post or at the first hearing, the CPS may not be involved at all. A private person may also instigate criminal proceedings.

Before we discuss criminal court procedure, we must first understand the classification of offences into summary, indictable and either way offences. Summary offences are triable by the magistrates only without committing the case for trial in the Crown Court. These are less serious crimes such as minor regulatory offences and motoring offences, for example, speeding, not obeying road signs and unauthorised parking. For some very minor offences, a defendant may be offered, and if not offered may ask for, permission to plead guilty by post. Indictable offences are usually more serious crimes, triable only in the Crown Court by a judge and a jury. Either way offences (or hybrid offences) are offences which may be tried either summarily in the magistrates' court or by indictment in the Crown Court.

Pre-trial procedure in magistrates' courts
All criminal cases start in the magistrates' courts. The procedure varies for different types of offence.

Summary offences
- The prosecution provides information to the court which will draft and serve a summons on the defendant requiring the defendant to attend the court hearing at a stated time and date.
- If offered by the prosecution, a defendant can plead guilty by post if the summary offence carries a maximum sentence of not more than three months imprisonment (s 12 of the Magistrates' Courts Act 1980). When pleading guilty by post, the defendant may also ask the court to consider mitigating circumstances before passing a sentence.
- At the hearing, the court clerk first reads out the charge and asks the defendant to plead guilty or not guilty.
- If the defendant pleads guilty, the magistrates will proceed to sentencing. If otherwise, the Court will proceed to trial if all parties are prepared, otherwise the hearing will be adjourned for preparation or for the attendance of witnesses.

Either way offences
- A defendant may be summoned to attend the first hearing on police bail or while being kept in custody by the police.
- The court clerk reads out the charge, then the court will ascertain whether the defendant has been informed of his right to receive advance information from the prosecution.
- The prosecution then represents details of the offence and the defendant makes his representation as well. The main purpose of this is for the magistrates to decide whether the case should be tried summarily or be sent for Crown Court trial, having considered their sentencing power.

- If summary trial is decided, the clerk will inform the defendant of his right for a jury trial in the Crown Court and that the magistrates may still commit him for sentencing in the Crown Court. If the defendant accepts a summary trial, the court will then take a plea. If the defendant pleads guilty, the court proceed with sentencing. Otherwise, the matter will proceed to trial or be adjourned. When adjourned, the magistrates will consider matters such as bail and legal aid. In January 2000, the government attempted to introduce a Bill to remove the defendant's right to opt for jury trials in either way offences but was defeated in the House of Lords. When the government re-introduce this again, a defendant will have no right to object if a magistrate decides on a summary trial; he only has a right to appeal.

- If the magistrates decide on a Crown Court trial, the defendant does not have a choice. Alternatively, if the defendant does not accept a summary trial, the case will be tried in the Crown Court. Before it is committed for Crown Court trial, the court has to conduct the so called committal proceedings, sometimes called preliminary or intermediate proceedings in the magistrates' courts. The purpose of this is for the prosecution to show that there is a *prima facie* case for the defendant to answer and a case for jury trial. If the prosecution fails to do this, the court may return a decision that the defendant has 'no case to answer' and will be released.

Indictable offences

The first appearance takes place in the magistrates' court when the defendant will only be required to confirm his name then the case will likely be adjourned for committal procedure. If it is decided that the defendant has a case to answer, the matter will be indicted for trial in the Crown Court. On this occasion, and at the earlier adjournment, the court will decide on bail and legal aid. We shall discuss bail next and criminal legal aid will be explained later together with civil legal aid.

Bail

We have come across police bail in an earlier section. In general, the police must consider bail once a person is charged. When the case proceeds to court, it is the magistrate and the judge in the Crown Court who consider bail, usually when the matter is adjourned. The Bail Act 1976 provides a general right to bail but it may not be granted if the offence is punishable with imprisonment and there are substantial grounds to believe that the defendant is likely to abscond (an example of supporting facts can be the defendant's previous bail record and uncertain address, etc), commit an offence, interfere with a witness or otherwise obstruct the course of justice. As a result, bail is not likely for serious crimes with strong prosecution evidence. Further, s 25 of the Criminal Justice and Public Order Act 1994 provides that bail shall be refused where the defendant is charged with, or convicted of, murder, attempted murder, manslaughter, rape, attempted rape, if previously convicted of such an offence or if the previous offence was manslaughter and a custodial sentence was imposed. Section 26 provides that a defendant need not be granted bail if the offence is indictable or triable either way and it appears to the court that he was on bail for earlier criminal proceedings at the date of the offence.

Bail can be unconditional. The only duty is for the defendant to surrender to custody of the court on an appointed date and time. Sureties (a sum of money provided by a third party securing the accused turning up at the court) and securities (the money provided by the defendant himself) may be required. This is conditional bail. Other conditions may be imposed such as curfew (not to go to certain places, for example, 100 yards within a battered girlfriend's residence), residence order (must stay in a certain place), report to the police and submission of passport. If bail is refused, or conditions are considered to be unreasonable, application can be made to a High Court Judge in chambers or the Crown Court for review.

Summary trial

Over 97% of criminal trials are summary trials at the magistrates' court. After the first hearing is conducted, and the defendant has pleaded not guilty, or summary trial is decided for an either way offence, the court will proceed with trial. The prosecution will present their case first then call their witnesses. This is called giving evidence in chief, during which time no leading questions are allowed. The defendant's solicitor can cross-examine (that is, be challenged by the defence lawyer) each witness who may then be re-examined by the prosecution lawyer. The purpose is to restore the quality of the evidence given. The defence will then present their case and call their witnesses, which may include the defendant himself. These witnesses can be again cross-examined and re-examined. Hearsay evidence is not admissible. A witness gives evidence stating what he saw and heard. If he starts telling the court what a third party told him, it is mere hearsay and the third party should testify, not him. Both sides then sum up their cases and the justices will announce their verdict. Before this, they may adjourn the case for them to consider the evidence in private or to discuss certain points of law with the legally trained justice's clerk. A justice's clerk advises the magistrates on law and procedure only and must not have input in deciding the verdict. If the decision is not guilty, the accused will be released. If it is guilty, then the court will proceed to sentencing or, if necessary, it will adjourn and order a report of the defendant to be prepared. Such a report may contain details regarding the person's mental, physical, social or other relevant personal circumstances. Before passing sentence the defence lawyer would likely raise some mitigating points aiming to persuade the magistrate to pass a less serious sentence. Ignorance of the law is not a defence but it can be a mitigating point. If this is the situation, the correct approach for an accused should be to plead guilty but to use his lack of knowledge and co-operation with the court for mitigation purposes.

In the magistrates' court, there can be two to a maximum of seven, most often three, magistrates on the bench hearing a case. A single magistrate may sit alone in either of the following situations:

- in minor cases involving very small fines or periods of imprisonment;
- when conducting a preliminary hearing; or
- when appointed as a stipendiary magistrate.

Apart from stipendiary magistrates who are full time paid magistrates, magistrates are laymen (see later section for the function and selection of magistrates). The logic is that crimes are committed against the people and are therefore tried by the people.

Trial on indictment

An indictment is a formal document setting out the charges and some particulars of the alleged crime. It is read out at the beginning of the trial before the defendant is asked to plead. If he pleads guilty, the court proceeds with sentencing. If he pleads not guilty, the court proceeds with the trial. The jury is sworn in. The prosecution gives its opening speech then calls its witnesses each to give evidence in chief by responding to the questions put to them by the prosecution. They will be cross-examined by the defence then re-examined by the prosecution. After all of the prosecution's evidence has been given, the defence opens its case. Similarly, defence witnesses are called, cross-examined and re-examined. Articles may be examined and experts' reports presented. Sometimes, the jury is taken to the crime scene in order to help them understand the case more thoroughly. The prosecution, and then the defence, will give their closing speeches. The judge will sum up the case, drawing the juries' attention to any important legal issues. In a jury trial, the judge deals with the law and the jury deals with the facts. The judge cannot assume the task of the jury and must not direct the jury to a verdict. The jury will then retire to consider its verdict. For criminal cases, the burden of proof is on the prosecution to prove beyond reasonable doubt that the defendant has committed the crime. The verdict is ideally decided by a unanimous vote of the jury. If after two hours of deliberation unanimity is not possible, the judge may direct that a majority verdict of 11:1 or 10:2 will be accepted. If the verdict is guilty, then the judge will proceed with sentencing. Again, the defence may raise some mitigating points and the judge may order a report regarding the convicted before sentencing. The report is particularly relevant if the mental condition of the convicted is an issue.

Sentencing

In magistrates' courts
There is a range of sentences that a magistrate can pass in a magistrates' court. They include absolute discharge, conditional discharge, fines, probation, community service orders, detention in a young offenders institution, imprisonment and suspended sentences. For motoring offences, the sentence can be disqualification from driving and points being endorsed on the convicted person's driving licence. A magistrate can also order for restitution (for example, return of the stolen goods), compensation, forfeiture of illegal materials and to pay the costs of the court. A magistrate does not have the power to pass a sentence of more than six months' imprisonment and/or a £5,000 fine for one single offence. For two or more offences, a sentence of up to twelve months' imprisonment may be given. However, if it comes to light that the offence is more serious than was originally thought, or that the convicted person's previous criminal record indicates that a heavy punishment should be ordered, the magistrate may commit the person to the Crown Court for sentencing.

In the Crown Court
If a person is found guilty, the judge will first hear evidence of his background, any previous convictions and any mitigation raised by the defence lawyer. Reports of the convicted person's condition may be ordered and other admitted offences can be taken into consideration. The range of sentence which can be passed in the Crown Court include:

- Death penalty (only for treason and for piracy with violence).
- Imprisonment and fully or partly suspended imprisonment. The Criminal Justice Act 1991 provides detail provisions for custodial sentence. In general, a custodial sentence should not be given unless no other punishments are justified or it is necessary to protect the public.
- Detention in a young offenders institution (for male offenders aged 14 to 21 and female offenders aged 15 to 21).
- Fines.
- Hospitalisation order.
- Community service.
- Probation.
- Motoring related punishments.
- Absolute or conditional discharge.

Similar to the magistrates' courts, the Crown Court can order for restitution, compensation, forfeiture and payment of the court's costs.

Criminal appeals
Some general rules:
- A convicted person may appeal against conviction and/or sentence. The prosecution has no general right of appeal against an acquittal. However, the Attorney General may, with leave of the Court of Appeal, refer a case to them where it appears that the sentence is unduly lenient.
- All appeals from the Magistrates' Court are heard by the Crown Court, usually in front of a judge and two to four magistrates. Section 1 of the Criminal Appeal Act 1995 provides that further appeals must either have leave (that is, permission) from the Court of Appeal or from the trial judge. With leave, an appeal can be made to the Court of Appeal then to the House of Lords, though the latter is very rare.
- With leave, an appeal against a Crown Court conviction can be brought to the Court of Appeal then again with leave to the House of Lords.
- Both the prosecution and convicted can appeal by way of case stated. This means that there is no dispute about the facts found but only an appeal against a point or points of law. This type of appeal is brought to the Divisional Court of the Queen's Bench Division

then with leave (only granted if there is an important point of law) further to the House of Lords.

- Section 3 of the Criminal Appeal Act 1995 repeals s 17 of the Criminal Appeal Act 1968, which provided that the Home Secretary could refer a Crown Court conviction to the Court of Appeal. Since 31 March 1997, much of this function is assumed by the Criminal Cases Review Commission.

- It should be noted that, when European or human rights law becomes an issue, the parties can bring the matter to the European Courts at almost anytime.

- In December 1999, the Lord Chancellor appointed Lord Justice Auld, a senior Judge of the Appeal, to report on criminal practices and procedures with a view to streamlining all their processes, increasing their efficiency and strengthening the effectiveness of their relationships with others across the whole of the criminal justice system. The report is due to be finalised by the end of 2000 and changes in practices and procedures are expected.

The civil process

Pre-trial procedure and the three litigation tracks

Lord Woolf (now appointed as Lord Chief Justice) was appointed in 1994 by the then Lord Chancellor, to conduct an inquiry into the civil justice system. On his proposal, the Civil Procedure Rules (CPR) 1998 were formed and took effect from 26 April 1999. The major aims of the reform were to improve access to justice, expedite the way cases were dealt with, reduce the cost of litigation and reduce the complexity of the rules. Under the new rules, the two tier system of High Court and county court was scrapped and a new single unified court system was created. Civil disputes are allocated into one of the three tracks: small claim, fast and multi-tracks. The new rules are subject to the overriding objective as set out in Pt 1 of the CPR. The objective is to enable the court to deal with cases justly which includes:

- ensuring that the parties are on an equal footing;

- saving expenses; and

- how the case can be dealt with expeditiously and fairly.

When the court exercises any discretion given to it or interprets the meaning of any rules, it will consider the factors such as:

- the amount of money involved;
- the complexity of the issues;
- the parties financial positions; and
- the proportionate use of the court's resources and public monies.

The courts are supposed to adopt a proactive case management role. The reform encourages out of court settlement and promotes the use of alternative dispute resolution.

It used to be the case that one could start a case either in the High Court or a county court. There was no financial limit to start a case. However, there were transfer criteria to decide in which court a case would be brought to its final trial. A writ was issued in the High Court, or one of its District Registries, and a summons was used in a county court. From 26 April 1999, there is only one procedure for a claimant (formerly, 'plaintiff') to start a case. A claimant should fill in a Particulars of Claim form and have it issued in any civil court with payment of an appropriate fee. He may choose to attach a Particulars of Claim stating the reason of the claim and the relief sought or to serve the form separately later on. The form is normally served by the court by first class post on the defendant who has 14 days after the service of the Particulars (not the Claim form) to reply. If the defendant files an acknowledgment of service, he has 28 days to reply. The defendant should respond by returning a form either to admit wholly or partly the claim or to deny the claim with or without a counterclaim. If nothing is done within these 14 or 28 days, the claimant can enter a judgment in default. If a defence is filed, the proceedings will be transferred to the defendant's home court. Statements of truth that should be signed by the parties or their solicitors must accompany all pleadings, that is, the Particulars of Claim, the Defence and Counterclaim and the Reply to the Defence. The statement of truth, which is a new concept under the new rules, declares that the parties honestly believe that the contents in the pleadings are true. The court now has wide powers to strike out any pleadings if it shows no reasonable grounds for bringing or defending a claim. The court will next send a form called Allocation Questionnaire to the parties. The answers to the questionnaire will help the procedural judge, usually a district judge, to allocate the claim to one of the three tracks. Both parties should file this questionnaire to the court in time and the claimant has to pay a further filing fee of £80 unless the claim is a money claim not exceeding £1,000.

The value of the claim is the main factor which determines which track to be allocated. Generally, if the value is no more than £5,000, the normal track is small claim. There are exceptions, for example (a) personal injury cases where general damages exceed £1,000 (general damages cover pain and suffering caused by the injury as opposed to special damages which are ascertainable in money terms such as loss of earnings and damaged car); and (b) residential tenants' claims for repairs exceeding £1,000. For a claim with value over £5,000 up to £15,000, the normal track is the fast track. If the case is a more complicated matter which may require that the trial will last for more than five hours, the case may be allocated to the multi-track. Multi-track is the normal track for any claim which does not fall in either of the other two tracks.

The next stage is the disclosure stage, in which the parties must disclose to the opponent any relevant documents that they hold. The idea is to confine only relevant documents to be used at the trial. The parties are then entitled to inspect the documents disclosed. There is generally no disclosure for the small claims. Once this 'paper chase' is complete, the case will be 'set down' for trial.

When the reform was at its proposal stage, the profession was sceptical about it. At the time of writing, the changes have been in force for almost one year and have been generally accepted to be a successful improvement.

Small claim hearing in the county court

The idea of the small claim track is to enable the court to dispose of small value or straightforward cases speedily and with the minimum of fuss. In the past, small claims were heard in chambers (that is, a meeting room in the court). Most hearings are now conducted in public but remain informal. The strict rules of evidence do not apply. The judge has wide powers to control the hearing and may ask questions of the parties and witnesses before allowing the parties or their advocates to do so. After listening to the parties and looking into the available evidence, the judge will make a decision and give his judgment. The new rules provide that, if a party has told the court at least seven days before the hearing of its intention not to attend, or if both parties have asked the court to decide the case in their absence, the court will do so and then send the parties a note of the judge's reasons for the decision made. This provision helps those whose personal attendance at the court would mean a lengthy and uneconomic journey.

Only very limited legal costs will be awarded in favour of the successful party, unless a party is proven to have behaved unreasonably. Out of pocket monies, for example, court fees, medical report fees and travelling costs are also recoverable. Any county court judgment will be registered with the County Court Judgment Registry, a public record, if the judgment remains wholly or partly unpaid within 28 days. This will adversely affect the credit rating of a defendant. If a defendant has satisfied the judgment, he should immediately inform the court of it. There is a limited right of appeal. The appellant has to prove either a serious irregularity has affected the proceedings or that the judge made a mistake of law.

Trials in other tracks and appeals

Trials in other tracks are more formal. Witnesses are subject to examination in chief, cross-examination and re-examination not too different from a criminal trial. Most civil cases are heard by a judge alone, who will determine the question of both law and fact. The judge will make his judgment on the balance of probabilities, in a practical sense, meaning that he believes in the facts presented by one party more than the other. Sometimes, judges want more time to examine the evidence and give judgment at a later hour or day. This is called a reserved judgment. Civil jury trials are rare but sometimes are available for cases such as defamation, malicious prosecution, false imprisonment and fraud.

The parties can generally bring an appeal to the Court of Appeal then, with leave of the court, can appeal further to the House of Lords. There is a special appeal route called the 'leap frog' procedure which is created by the Administration of Justice Act 1969. Here, a High Court case can leap frog the Court of Appeal and make an appeal directly to the House of Lords. In order to use this appeal process, the parties must agree and the trial judge must issue a certificate that the case is one of public importance and that it concerns statutory interpretation or the decision is bound by a previous decision of the House itself. Further, the House of Lords must give leave to the appeal.

Legal aid and advice

Legal aid

Recently, there have been fundamental changes to the legal aid system. The Legal Services Commission replaced the Legal Aid Board from 1 April 2000. It used to be the case that a solicitors' firm could carry out all types of legal advice under various legal aid schemes as long as it was registered with the Legal Aid Board. Legal aid schemes are now all subject to franchise and law firms can only give legally aided advice in relation to a particular franchise category that they hold. The categories are consumer and general contract, crime, debt, employment, housing, immigration, matrimonial, mental health, personal injury and welfare benefit. The various Legal Services Commission schemes include:

Legal help and help at court scheme

This scheme generally covers up to two hours legal help by a solicitor. Three hours work is provided for in family proceedings if the solicitor drafts a divorce petition on behalf of the client. The solicitor's charge is paid for by the Legal Services Commission's funds. If property or money is recovered or preserved for the client, the solicitor will charge for his costs on the property or money. The work under this scheme must be concerned with a matter of English law and may include initial advice, writing letters for the client, negotiating on the client's behalf, preparing a case and so forth. It, however, does not cover representation in court or at tribunals. Nor does it cover conveyancing and will matters unless there are some special circumstances. When a person requires help under this scheme, he should first make an appointment with a solicitors' firm which is franchised for his type of problem. At the beginning of the appointment, the solicitor will assist the client to complete a form and assess the eligibility of the client to receive this free advice. To be eligible, a person's disposable income, currently, must not exceed £84 per week. Disposable Income is the person's income with deductions of income tax, National Insurance contributions and an allowance depending on the number of dependants. The person's disposable capital should not exceed the prescribed amount of £1,000. Disposable capital means savings, investments, valuable possessions (for example, jewellery) with a deduction of an allowance depending on the number of dependants.

The capital value of the person's home is usually ignored unless the market value less the amount outstanding (maximum £100,000) has exceeded £100,000. People on Income Support, Income Based Jobseeker's Allowance or who receive the maximum tax credit under the Working Families or Disabled Person's Tax Credit are automatically qualified on income but their disposable capital must still be assessed.

Assistance by Way of Representation

Assistance by Way of Representation (ABWOR) is a scheme which covers the costs of a solicitor preparing a client's case and representing him in certain civil hearings, but it is only available where the case falls within one of the franchise categories of matrimonial, crime or debt. It is also available to patients appearing before the Mental Health Review Tribunals and to prisoners facing disciplinary charges.

Extended legal help

Where further help is required for a person who is involved in litigation, he may be advised to apply for legal aid. The previous civil legal aid has now been replaced by the Community Legal Service and the previous criminal legal aid will be replaced by the Criminal Defence Service.

Community Legal Service (previously civil legal aid)

The Legal Services Commission must be satisfied that the applicant has a good enough case (that is, the merits test) and is financially eligible (that is, the means test) before a person is awarded with this higher level of legal help.

The merits test

The applicant has to show that he has reasonable grounds for taking, defending or being a party to a court action. Factors to be considered include:

- reasonable case?;
- reasonable award?;
- does the applicant need a lawyer?

An applicant may have a good case but if the award were only estimated to be about £200, then it would not be reasonable to spend £2,000 public fund to support the case. If a client has a rightful debt against a company which has gone out of business, again, the Commission would not likely support such a case. Legal aid is not generally available for defamation, small claims and tribunal cases except for matters in the Land Tribunal and Employment Appeal Tribunal. There is a tendency that 'no win no fee' arrangements are encouraged to take on personal injury cases and, therefore, the merits test for such cases is becoming increasingly more stringent.

The means test

If the applicant is on low income with little capital, his case may qualify for free funding. If he is better off, he may be asked to pay a contribution to the costs. People on Income Support, Income Based Jobseeker's Allowance or who receive the maximum tax credit under the Working Families or Disabled Person's Tax Credit may automatically qualify. Generally, people whose disposable income does not exceed £2,725 per annum will also qualify for free help. For people with disposable income between £2,725 to £8,067 per annum, a contribution will be required. With a disposable income of over £8,067, the person will not be eligible for the scheme. Regarding disposable capital, no contribution is required for under £3,000. For £3,000 to £6,750, a contribution will be required. Over £6,750, the person will not be eligible. Again, if any property or money is recovered or preserved for the client with the help of the Community Legal Service funding, the client may be asked to put some or all of this money towards the solicitor's costs. This is called the 'Statutory Charge'. Where this applies, the Community Legal Service funding acts as a loan. There are plans to simplify these eligibility tests; the way people are assessed as to whether they receive civil aid may change in the not too distant future.

Criminal legal aid

There is a 24 hour duty solicitor scheme which runs throughout England and Wales at police stations to ensure that people who are arrested can obtain legal advice either in person or over the telephone. There is also a duty solicitor scheme at court whereby people attending court who do not have appropriate legal representation can obtain free advice from the duty solicitor. These schemes are not subject to a means test.

Criminal legal aid will be replaced by the Criminal Defence Service which is not in place yet. Criminal legal aid application is usually made to the magistrate's clerk either in writing or orally prior to a hearing. The condition is that the court must make a legal aid order where it appears that it is in the interest of justice; that legal aid should be granted; and that the applicant requires financial help. Issues relating to interest of justice include:

- whether the accused would be in danger of losing his liberty or job;
- whether there would be a possible serious damage to the accused's reputation;
- whether there is a substantial question of law in the case;
- the accused may be mentally ill.

The financial criteria are that no contribution is required if disposable income is, currently, less than £53 per week and disposable capital has not exceeded £3,000. There is no upper financial limit for criminal legal aid. The clerk considers all the factors and criteria then, usually, it is the magistrate who makes the legal aid order at the end of a hearing.

Legal advice

The Community Legal Service (CLS) was formally launched at the beginning of April 2000. A key part of the new system is the formations of CLS partnerships between the Legal Services Commission, legal advice bodies, local authorities and other funders. The functions of the partnerships include the co-ordination of funding and delivery of the legal help service. They set up local advice networks which include lawyers, Citizens Advice Bureaux, law centres and local councils. The idea is to provide a 'one stop legal shop' for poorer members of the community who need legal help. It used to be the case that the work of the above mentioned organisations were quite separate.

The Legal Services Commission aims to have a CLS network up and running in almost every area of England and Wales by the end of March 2002. By that time, when someone needs legal help, he should be able to approach any of the advisory organisations or a franchised law firm. If an advisor thinks that it is more appropriate for another organisation within the partnership to deal with the matter, he is supposed to draft a note outlining the client's circumstances and refer him to another organisation. This way, the client does not need to explain his situation to another advisor again and time and costs will be saved. If the person does not know where to get help or may only want some straight forward information to begin with, he can approach a so called CLS information point. In time, there will be more and more information points in libraries and other public places where the person can obtain initial information and find out where to go for further advice. The CLS publishes a directory which lists all the lawyers, advice centres and many other organisations which are associated with the CLS. This directory is not only available at the information points but also at the website www.justask.org.uk. One can also phone the CLS helpline at 0845 6081122 (charged at local rate), or other numbers established from time to time, to find out how to get in touch with one of the CLS providers.

Apart from legal advisors who are directly associated with CLS, there are places where a person can obtain free or low cost legal advice. They include:

- *Fixed fee interview*

  Many solicitors' firms operate a low fixed fee first interview scheme. Such firms can be found in The Law Society's Local Solicitors Directory, the CLS directory and the Yellow Pages.

- *Accident Line scheme*

  The Law Society also operates this scheme. Solicitors taking part offer a free first interview for anyone who has suffered injury or illness after an accident. Apart from looking up the mentioned directories, one can also call the Accident Line free.

- *Conditional fees*

  This is a new way of funding legal costs mostly used in personal injury cases. If a person has to take his case to court, some lawyers are now prepared to accept a 'no win no fee' arrangement. This means that if the claimant loses the case he will not have to pay for his solicitor's work. If he wins, he may have to pay a so called 'success fee' which contains a percentage increase of the usual legal costs, up to a maximum of 100% as agreed between the client and his solicitor. There is usually an insurance premium required for such an arrangement. In the event that a claimant loses, he will normally be ordered to pay the defendant's legal costs then the insurers will pick up the bill. The Access to Justice Act 1999 has now made it possible for the winning party to recover the success fee and the insurance premium from the losing party.

- *Other advice*

  There is other free or low cost advice available, such as legal service of a trade union for its members; other organisations, like the AA, RAC, the Federation of Small Businesses, also offer legal help to their members. Sometimes, some household or car insurance policies provide helplines or actually cover legal expenses.

Legal institutions

Lord Chancellor's Department

Discussion of the court system should start from the Lord Chancellor's Department, whose essential function is to promote a fair, efficient and effective administration of justice in England and Wales. The minister responsible for the Department is the Lord Chancellor, currently Lord Irvine of Lairg, who is also the head of the legal profession and judiciary. His main responsibilities are:

- to maintain an effective management of the courts and a number of tribunals;
- to appoint and to advise on the appointment of judges, magistrates and other judicial office holders;
- to administer legal aid;
- to promote the reform and revision of the legal system and law.

The Department's estate comprises of over 400 buildings, ranging from the Royal Courts of Justice in the Strand, London, to small court offices in more remote areas in England and Wales. The Department used to administer its courts directly but, since April 1995, this role has been taken by a separate executive agency, the Court Service Agency. One of the major exceptions are the magistrates' courts which are locally administered, although the Lord Chancellor is accountable to Parliament for their operation. Magistrates' courts are financed by the local authorities which reclaim the majority of their expenditure from the Department.

High judicial office

The Lord Chancellor is the nominal head of the House of Lords and the chairman of the Judicial Committee of the Privy Council. The House, on its judicial function, consists of nine to 12 Lords of Appeal in Ordinary (commonly called Law Lords) and other Lords who hold, or held, high judicial office. Currently, there are 15 of these other Lords who are eligible to hear appeals in the House, but once they reach the age of 75, they are no longer eligible. The Judicature Acts 1873–75 created the Court of Appeal and, from 1966, the court was divided into two divisions, civil and criminal, when the Criminal Appeal Act 1966 came into force. The Court of Appeal (Civil Division) is headed by the Master of the Rolls who is also the head of The Law Society. The Lord Chief Justice presides over the Court of Appeal (Criminal Division). The Court of Appeal consists of a maximum of 32 Lord Justices of Appeal, each of whom specialises in different areas of law, some hearing appeals on civil, some on criminal matters and some on both.

The theory of separation of powers (that is, legislative, executive and judicial powers) is supposed to be a sound structure for a State and a safeguard for democracy. In Britain, we cannot say that we are anywhere near to the full exercise of this theory. The Lord Chancellor is a member of the government, his appointment is political rather than judicial. From magistrates to judges, appointments are made by the Lord Chancellor upon the recommendations of local regions or judicial colleagues. For higher judicial office, the Lord Chancellor always obtains an agreement from the Prime Minister before any appointments. It is often said that, in Britain, judicial and political powers will never be completely separate.

The courts and their composition

Magistrates' courts

Magistrates are also known as 'justices of the peace'. Their history dates back to the end of the 12th century. Their task was to act as 'guardians of the peace' in their local areas. In the modern age, magistrates' courts have been developed to play a major part in the administration of criminal law. All criminal litigation starts in magistrates' courts and over 97% of criminal trials take place there. They also have jurisdiction on some civil matters such as licensing applications and prosecuting civil debts for certain authorities. There are about 900 magistrates' courts in England and Wales situated in every county and most boroughs. At present, they are run by about 100 separate regional magistrates' court committees consisting almost entirely of local magistrates. There are plans to reduce the number of committees to improve efficiency. Functionally, a magistrates' court can be divided into four areas:

The court of petty sessions

Magistrates sit in the court of petty sessions to hear trials of summary offences and either way offences tried in the magistrates' court. Magistrates sitting in this court have a limited power of sentencing (see previous sections for details).

The court of committal proceedings

Committal proceedings in the magistrates' court are also known as 'preliminary hearings'. It examines the preliminary evidence presented by the prosecution to see if they review a *prima facie* case for a jury trial. Jury trial is not cheap and it requires the attendance of jurors, normally 12 per hearing. Criminal conviction has to be proven beyond reasonable doubt. If the prosecution's evidence appears to be very thin, there will be a slim chance for conviction so the case should be thrown out at this stage.

The youth court

The youth court in the magistrates' court was created by the Children and Young Persons Act 1933 to try persons under 18 years of age. They are separated from the normal courts and are held at least one hour before or after the adult hearing. The public is not allowed to attend and the press are restricted. The name of the accused is not publishable. Cases are heard by three magistrates not all of the same sex and, by the Criminal Justice Act 1991, the parents of a child aged 16 years or less must attend with their child and the parents of older minors may also be required to attend.

There are a range of sentences which may be passed including:

- fines;
- binding over order against the parents who will promise that their child will not commit another crime within a set period of time. If that happens, the parents will have to pay the ordered sum;
- probation;
- care order by which the offender is committed to secure local authority accommodation and the parental responsibilities are transferred to the local authority;
- hospital or guardianship order;
- attendance centre order for training;
- custodial sentence, which is the detention in a young offender's institution only when no other option is justified or it is necessary to protect the public.

The law regards children of under 10 years of age to be incapable of committing a crime. Therefore, no child under this age can be subjected to a criminal trial. However, children whose parents fail to control them and who cause continuous grievances and damages to others, for which older children could be convicted, can have care orders issued to them by the magistrates' courts. For 10 to 14 year olds, the prosecution must prove an extra *mens rea* of mischievous discretion on top of the normal *mens rea* of the offence. Mischievous discretion means that the child knows that the offending act is seriously wrong. Minors over 14 years of age are fully liable in crime; however, they are dealt with in the youth court described above.

Civil jurisdiction in the magistrates' court

Examples of this include:

- the enforcement of certain civil debts of some public bodies, such as unpaid council tax, gas, electricity and water bills;
- certain family and matrimonial matters, such as jurisdiction relating to protection against domestic violence, committing children to the care of the local authority and adoption and guardianship applications;
- the granting and renewing of licences for applications, such as on and off licence for pubs, restaurants and off licensed shops, betting and gaming licences and theatre and cinematography licences. In these applications, the magistrates are generally asked to consider two main issues: whether the premises are suitable and whether the applicant is a suitable person to be granted the licence.

Crown Court

The Crown Court tries indictable offences and offences triable either-way for which the magistrates' courts have committed for Crown Court trial. The courts are situated in 89 court centres in England and Wales. The larger centres do not only hear Crown Court cases but also High Court and county court matters. In London, the Crown Court is called the Central Criminal Court and is commonly known as the Old Bailey. Trials are heard by a judge and a jury. The judge deals with the law and the jury decides on the facts. A judge can be a High Court Judge, a circuit judge or a recorder. Recorders are part time judges, being barristers or solicitors of at least 10 years' standing. Recorders should be committed to serve not less than one month of work in the Crown Court each year.

County courts

The county courts were established by the County Courts Act 1846 for the purpose of providing quick and inexpensive relief for small civil disputes. There are 270 county courts in England and Wales. Apart from general civil matters, the county courts play a major role in divorce and divorce related matters, that is, financial settlement and children. Judicially, county courts consist of district judges and circuit judges. District judges are barristers or solicitors of at least seven years' general qualifications and they conduct the day to day management of cases. They also hear interlocutory applications and cases in the small claim track. England and Wales are divided into six circuits and there are approximately 125 circuit judges. Circuit judges are either barristers with at least 10 years experience or solicitors with at least seven years standing. When directed by the Lord Chancellor, High Court Judges and recorders may try county court cases.

High Court

There is only one High Court in England and Wales. This is why, traditionally, High Court terms begin with capital letters while county court terms do not. It sits in the Royal Courts of Justice in London. When it sits in other centres, those centres are called District Registries of the High Court. The High Court consists of three divisions each hearing different types of cases. These are:

The Queen's Bench Division

Headed by the Lord Chief Justice, the Queen's Bench Division deals with matters such as tort, contract and personal injury. There are also two specialist courts here, namely, the Admiralty Court, which deals with marine disputes, and the Commercial Court, which handles commercial disputes, particularly banking, insurance and agency matters. The Family Division is presided over by the President. They hear non-contentious probate, applications concerning children such as guardianship and wardship and petitions regarding marriage such as validity of marriage. The third is the Chancery Division, which is headed by the Vice Chancellor. This division is concerned with matters such as property law, trusts, company law, partnership disputes, insolvency and contentious probate. However, one should note that these Divisions do not have exclusive jurisdiction to hear the matters listed above. County courts hear these cases too. With the New Civil Procedure Rules, civil cases allocated to the High Court are likely to be those proceeding in the multi-track. The High Court also hears appeals such as those from certain administrative tribunals, Inland Revenue decisions and the Solicitors Disciplinary Tribunal hearings. High Court judges are called *'puisne* judges'. Different judges specialise in different areas of law. Some *puisne* judges only hear civil cases and some only sit in the Crown Court. In a civil court, the judge sits alone. Lord Justices of Appeal in the Court of Appeal, circuit judges and recorders from the county court may sometimes be assigned to hear cases in the High Court.

Court of Appeal (Civil and Criminal Division)
The judicial composition in the Court of Appeal is discussed above, in an earlier section on high judicial office.

The Court of Appeal (Civil Division) hears appeals from the High Court, the county courts and various tribunals such as the Land Tribunal and the Employment appeal Tribunal. The Criminal Division deals with appeals from the Crown Court against conviction or sentence. The prosecution does not have a general right of appeal against acquittal, but the Attorney General can refer cases to the Division where he feels that the sentence imposed was unduly lenient. Further, the Criminal Cases Review commission have now assumed the function of referring cases to the Court of Appeal after a conviction on indictment or on a finding of not guilty by reason of insanity.

Cases in both divisions are normally dealt with by three, five or seven higher judges (that is, the Master of the Rolls, Lord Chief Justice and the Lord Justices of Appeal). Sometimes, Lords from the House of Lords, the President and Vice Chancellor from the High Court hear cases in this bench. Decisions are on majority vote. The reasons given form the *ratio decidendi* and the principle given by the dissenting judges become *obiter dicta*.

The House of Lords
The House of Lords is the final court of appeal for the whole of the UK in civil cases and for England, Wales and Northern Ireland for criminal cases. The House hears appeals from the Court of Appeal, 'leap frog' appeals from the High Court and appeals direct from the Divisional Court of the Queen's Bench Division by way of case stated. There is no general right of appeal. Leave to appeal has to be granted by the House or the earlier court. For civil matters, the case must be one of public importance and for criminal appeals the issues must be based on a point of law. Cases are heard by three, five or seven Law Lords or other Lords who hold, or have held, high judicial office. Very occasionally, the Lord Chancellor may sit as a member on the bench. The Lords however will lose their eligibility to hear cases once they

reach 75 years of age. Decisions are made on majority vote. Since the practice statement issued by Lord Gardiner in 1966, the House of Lords is not bound by its own past decisions leaving more room for the common law to grow and change with the times.

Other courts and tribunals

Privy Council

The Judicial Committee of the Privy Council's main work is to hear the final appeals from The Isle of Man and the Channel Islands, British Colonies and Protectorates and those Commonwealth Countries who do not handle their final appeals. The Lord Chancellor and the Law Lords sit in this court and the procedure is similar to that in the House of Lords. Their decisions are immensely persuasive in practice but do not bind the English courts in principle.

Coroners' court

This court deals with inquests on violent or unnatural deaths, deaths from an unknown cause and death in prison. The coroners also have jurisdiction concerning treasure troves. The management of the coroners' courts is the responsibility of the Home Secretary not the Lord Chancellor.

Tribunals

Apart from ordinary courts, certain legislation provides for the creation of tribunals to decide on the particular scope of those statutes. There are now over 50 of these statutory tribunals and the common ones include:

- Industrial Tribunals hear employment related disputes such as unfair dismissal, redundancies, sex and race discrimination at work, equal pay and maternity pay.
- Social Security Appeals Tribunals hear disputes relating to social benefits.
- Rent Tribunals hear disputes between landlords and tenants.
- Land Tribunals decide on valuation of certain interests relating to land, such as the amount of compensation when local authorities compulsorily purchase land.

There are also domestic tribunals. These deal with matters concerned with internal regulation of an organisation rather than the implementation of public statutes. The important tribunals in this category are those created by professional organisations, such as the Professional Conduct Committee of the General Medical Council and the Solicitors Disciplinary Tribunal. Appeals from Tribunals like these can be brought to the ordinary court system.

The purpose of tribunals is to help in administering the legislation which created them efficiently and inexpensively. The hearings are less formal and, generally, legal representation is not required. In a way, they also help to reduce the pressure of work in the ordinary courts. Another advantage of tribunals is that cases are heard by people who have practical experience in particular fields.

Personnel of the law

Laymen in the law

Juries

Crown court trials are tried by a judge and a jury. Juries also hear matters in the coroners' courts. In civil courts, matters such as defamation, malicious prosecution, false imprisonment and some fraud cases can be tried by jury. High Court and Crown Court juries normally consist of 12 jurors while the normal number of jurors in county courts is only eight.

Jurors are supposed to be randomly selected. A juror must be aged between 18 and 70, on the electoral role and have been resident in UK for the last five years. If a person has previously been sentenced to prison for five years or longer, he is disqualified for life. There are others who cannot be called to serve as a juror, they are persons who:

- have served any prison sentence, youth custody, borstal detention or have been given a suspended sentence within the last 10 years;
- have been placed on probation within the last five years;
- have a mental disorder; or
- are concerned with the administration of justice and the clergy.

When a person is selected, it is an offence not to attend. There are excuses as of right which include having served as a juror within the past two years; being over 65; being a doctor or a member of some other medical profession; being an MP or a full time member of Her Majesty's armed forces. A person can also be temporarily deferred for other reasons such as physical disability; limited knowledge of English; or any other valid reason, one of the most common is having booked a holiday. A jury's verdict is decided by a unanimous vote. If after two hours of deliberation unanimity is not possible, the judge may accept an 11:1 or 10:2 majority verdict.

Magistrates and their clerks

Lay magistrates are nominated by regional committees and appointed by the Lord Chancellor on behalf of the Queen. The aim is to have a good cross-section of people of good character and achievement in all walks of life on the bench. The only requirement is that they reside within 15 miles of the area. They are not paid for their work on the bench, but do receive expenses. They are not required to be legally qualified but have to attend training courses. The idea is that suspects are tried by their own fellow citizens who represent the local community and who have intimate knowledge of the local area. There are currently approximately 30,000 magistrates in England and Wales. Another type of magistrate is the stipendiary magistrate, who is a full time, paid magistrate. They are barristers or solicitors of at least seven years' standing and are appointed by the Lord Chancellor. They work in larger cities and towns where caseloads are heavy and crimes tend to be more sophisticated. There are approximately 90 stipendiary magistrates and about half of them sit in London courts.

Magistrates are helped by legally qualified justices' clerks. In court, the clerk advises the justices on points of law and procedure, make records of the proceedings and administer legal aid. There is one thing they must not do which is to give any input when the magistrates consider their verdict. Out of court and with their colleagues, they train magistrates and manage the day to day running of the courts.

There has been much debate regarding jury trials in recent months. This has been fuelled by the defeat, in the House of Lords, of the government's attempt to introduce a Bill to remove the defendant's right to opt for a jury trial in either way offences and the government's determination to bring about the change. The Bill, if reintroduced, would allow only magistrates to decide where trials would take place, though a defendant would have the right to appeal. The government relied on an earlier report which concluded, from a sample of 977 cases, that 60% of defendants who elected jury hearings pleaded guilty at the beginning of their Crown Court trials and argues that this leads to extra cost, police time being wasted and greater inconvenience and worry to victims and witnesses. The government also predicts savings of around £105 million per year in which £66 million would come from reduced prison costs as a result of shorter sentences being passed by magistrates. This reform will come about sooner or later so the issue may well be whether the magistrate's court can cope with the change and how they should be prepared for it. Civil liberties lawyers would condemn the magistracy as 'white, middle class and middle aged, sitting in judgment on young, working class and often black defendants'. A greater danger might be that they can easily become 'case hardened'. The other side of the argument is that lay magistracy is far more socially diverse than it has been portrayed. Statistics show that the representation of ethnic minorities is far more impressive. If the change has to come, these trends should, at the same time, be maintained and improved, then defendants will be satisfied that they still have a 'jury' which may be on a small scale, consisting of three magistrates.

Legal professions

Barristers
There are two main bodies of lawyers in our legal system – barristers and solicitors. Barristers are often called counsel. There are about 9,000 barristers in England and Wales. Their main work is to conduct cases in courts and to draft pleadings and opinion for litigation. With 10 years' experience, they can apply to become Queen's Counsel (that is, QC, to take silk). Their governing body is the Bar Council (that is, the General Council of the Bar). Its function is to lay down general policies, promote and uphold the standards, honour and independence of the profession. It also has certain disciplinary powers. Together with the Inns of Court, the Bar Council is also involved in training barristers. All judges of the superior courts are barristers. There have been a few solicitors appointed as High Court judges but this is still very rare.

To become a barrister, one should first obtain a law degree or pass the Common Professional Examination, which is not an independent qualification itself but is recognised by the legal profession as if a bachelor degree holder of other discipline has a law degree. The person should then become a student at one of the four Inns of Court, that is, Lincoln's Inn, Gray's Inn, Inner Temple and Middle Temple, to receive training and to pass the Bar Vocational Course. They have to keep terms (that is, dine in their Inns) as well. Since September 1997, some Vocational Courses have been offered outside London. The person then has to become a pupil in barristers' chambers as a trainee for one year, after which time the person is a fully qualified barrister.

Solicitors

There are about 73,000 practising solicitors, of which 55,000 work in private practices (that is, law firms as opposed to in house solicitors or other organisations). Solicitors have a much wider work scope than barristers, but the majority of their work involves conveyancing; commercial leases; drafting contracts; wills and probate matters; advising on business and company law; matrimonial problems; and civil and criminal litigation, mainly on the procedural side. For advocacy, especially in higher courts or in trials, they would often issue instructions to counsels. However, solicitors do have rights of audience in tribunals, magistrates' courts, county courts, Crown Court if it is an appeal or a sentencing hearing committed from a magistrates' court. Solicitors only have a very limited right to advocate on behalf of a client in the High Court and have no such right at all in more superior courts unless an advocacy certificate is obtained (see below).

The governing body is The Law Society which organises the admission, education and training of solicitors. All practising solicitors contribute to a Compensation Fund maintained by The Law Society, from which clients can be repaid their losses caused by the default or neglect of solicitors. In September 1996, the former Solicitors' Complaints Bureau was replaced by the Office for the Supervision of Solicitors (OSS), which is supposed to be a separate organisation but is still set up by The Law Society. Any complaints are initially made to the OSS but could ultimately be brought to the Solicitors Disciplinary Tribunal which has the power to impose fines, suspend a solicitor or completely strike a solicitor off the roll (that is, the register of solicitors). Generally, a client cannot instruct a barrister directly and must do so through a solicitor.

To become a solicitor, a person has to first obtain a law degree or pass the Common Professional Examination. He has to attend a one year Legal Practice Course, then pass the examination at the end. He shall then enter into a training contract to become a trainee in a firm of solicitors or a recognised legal department in a company or an organisation (for example, government office) for two years. During the traineeship, he has to attend Professional Skills Courses after which he will become a fully qualified solicitor.

Although lawyers tend to specialise on one aspect of legal work (solicitors or barristers), even in countries which have only one single legal profession, there are some arguments regarding the two bodies system in the English system. One of these is that clients normally end up paying two fees. It can, nevertheless, be counter argued that the opportunity of having obtained a second opinion is directly or indirectly promoted by the system and this is particularly valuable for cases which are not straightforward. Another argument is that communication between two lawyers could sometimes cause inefficiency. However, this can be avoided if a solicitor and a counsel can establish an understanding that unnecessary formalities are disposed of. Barristers used to have exclusive right of audience in the higher courts. This has been changed since December 1993 by the Courts and Legal Services Act 1990 which allows solicitors to obtain full right of audience in the High Court, Crown Court, Court of Appeal and House of Lords after having undergone certain training to obtain advocacy certificates. However, applications from solicitors have been slow. By the Spring of 2000, six years on, only about 150 out of 55,000 solicitors practising in private firms have qualified for advocacy in all proceedings, about 750 for criminal proceedings and approximately 170 for civil proceedings. There have been plans to simplify the procedure and to encourage solicitors to obtain the certificates. This may encourage law students to train as solicitors rather than barristers. Nevertheless, it cannot be said that this is a 'major step' towards the abandonment of the two tier system.

Immunity from negligence claim

Judges and witnesses in legal proceedings have immunity from an action of negligence. It used to be the case that barristers were not liable in negligence for their advocacy in court and for matters which occurred beforehand and were intimately connected with how the case was conducted (*Rondel v Worsley* (1969)). This immunity covered similar aspects of work carried out by solicitors, but the extent of the immunity was never too clear. The justifications for the immunity were suggested to be:

- a duty of care to a client might conflict with an advocate's duty to the court and to the administration of justice;
- in theory, barristers could not choose their clients;
- a court of competent jurisdiction should not be challenged directly or indirectly, otherwise its authority would be undermined.

In the recent case of *Hall v Simmons* (2000), which was heard in the House of Lords in July 2000, the seven member House brought to an end this advocate's immunity, holding that the immunity is no longer supported by public policy and that it has ceased to exist in both civil and criminal cases. A minority of three agreed that immunity is redundant in civil cases, but thought that it should continue in criminal cases. This decision has finally clarified the confusions associated with the immunity and puts solicitors on an equal footing with barristers, so that apportionment of liability in negligence claims arising from the conduct of litigation can be dealt with sensibly.

Legal executives

Legal executives are governed by The Institute of Legal Executives (ILEX) which was established in 1963 to give professional status to those who work in solicitors' offices but who have not been trained as solicitors. There are courses to attend (part time or full time), examinations to pass and a period of apprenticeship to serve for a legal executive to become a fully qualified fellow of the Institute. This process can be as long as seven to eight years. A fellow can take further examinations to become a solicitor.

The law officers

The Attorney General is an MP who is, usually, an experienced barrister. The appointment is a political one and the Attorney General's duties include:

- representing the Crown in civil cases;
- prosecuting in certain criminal matters;
- being the head of the Bar Council;
- supervising the work of the Director of Public Prosecutions (DPP); and
- advising the government on legal issues.

The Solicitor General is the deputy to the Attorney General. This is also a political appointment. The DPP is a civil servant appointed by the Attorney General and is the head of the Crown Prosecution Service.

Index

171

#0080 - 250618 - C0 - 234/156/10 - PB - 9781859415436